# Readers' Favorites COOKBOOK

## Favorite Paleo, Primal & Grain-Free Recipes

BY PALEO MAGAZINE AND AMAZING MEMBERS
OF THE PALEO COMMUNITY

**Paleo Media Group**
Bend, Oregon

www.PaleoMediaGroup.com

First Published in 2013 by Paleo Media Group LLC
www.PaleoMediaGroup.com

ISBN 13: 978-0-9887172-2-0

Book design by Kate Miller, Kate Miller Design (www.KateMillerDesign.com)

Food photography on pages 59, 65, 69, 73, 75, 77, 79, 81, 91, 95, 97, 99, 101, 107, 109, 115, 117, 119,
121, 123, 127, 129, 131, 133, 137, 139, 141, 143, 145, 149, 153, 155, 159, 161, 163, 165, 167
by Savannah Wishart (www.PrimalRevolutions.com)

Beginning chapters by Tony Federico (www.FitnessInAnEvolutionaryDirection.com)

Printed in USA

This book is a collaborative effort that was only made possible by the amazing contributions from the following individuals.

We would like to thank Tony Federico (www.FitnessInAnEvolutionaryDirection.com) for eagerly accepting the task of putting together the beginning chapters of this book. Tony did an outstanding job of weaving a story of how the idea of eating together began, the importance of this ritual, and why it's incredibly important to maintain these traditions today. This set the feel of the entire book and laid the perfect foundation for the recipes that follow.

A big thank you to Savannah Wishart (www.PrimalRevolutions.com), photographer extraordinaire, for working, again, with a tight deadline while producing absolutely stunning, mouth-watering photos of some of the recipes in this book.

A huge thank you to the Paleo community! We are constantly in awe of how amazing this community is and were overwhelmed by the response to our call for recipes, and personal stories, when putting this book together. It's extremely motivating to see how others are improving their lives and we are forever grateful to everyone who submitted to be a part of this project. Thank you!

# thank you.

TABLE OF CONTENTS

# BREAKFASTS

CRANBERRY ORANGE MACADAMIA SCONES
66

MORNING EGG MUFFINS
74

84

QUICK BREAKFAST SAUSAGE

PALEO BREAKFAST COOKIES
109

APPLESAUCE STRAWBERRY OMELET
141

157

CINNAMON SQUARE CRUNCH CEREAL

# ENTRÉES

BALSAMIC MARINATED SKIRT STEAK W/ PEACH MANGO SALSA
60

COCONUT CHICKEN STRIPS
64

68

ITALIAN MEATBALLS
72

PALEO CHICKEN WINGS
78

PALEO GARDEN BURGER
80

82

PORK TENDERLOIN W/ HEARTY SPICE RUB

ASIAN CHICKEN SOUP
93

EASY CRAB SOUP

99

AUTUMN TURKEY SALAD

FENNELLED PALEO CHICKEN
101

103

MOROCCAN MEATBALLS

BEEF BACK RIBS
105

PALEO BROCCOLI BEEF
115

121

ULTIMATE PALEO PAD THAI

123

CHICKEN & SAUSAGE JAMBALAYA

127

COSTA RICAN CEVICHE

GROUND BEEF SKILLET
129

PERSIAN SLOW COOKER LAMB
131

ROASTED HALIBUT WITH GREEN OLIVE RELISH
137

BISON "SLIDERS"
139

143

ZUCCHINI PASTA WITH AVOCADO CREAM SAUCE

SWEET APPLE RABBIT SKEWERS
145

153

BAKED PORK RIBS

PALEOISTA'S WILD SALMON, EGGS, KALE & AVOCADO
155

STOVETOP TANDOORI CHICKEN
163

LAMB SLIDERS
165

# SIDES

BAKED CINNAMON, FENNEL AND PEARS
**58**

BEET & MARROW SOUP
**62**

KALE SALAD
**107**

**111**
SPICY GRILLED STUFFED AVOCADO

**56**

BACONY-Y BABA GHANOUSH

BRAISED BACON BRUSSELS SPROUTS
**149**

**161**

FAST GREEN EASY

# SAUCES/DIPS/DRESSING

PALEO-FRIENDLY MAYO
**95**

SPICY AVOCADO DRESSING
**119**

RED PEPPER DIP
**133**

# BAKING/DESSERTS/SNACKS/BEVERAGES

**54**
ALMOND BUTTER BARK

**70**
GREEN SMOOTHIE

NUT FREE NO'OAT GRANOLA
**76**

SEA SALT & CHIVE CRACKERS
**86**

BERRY SHORTCAKES & WHIPPED CREAM
**91**

**97**
CINNAMON CRUMBLE COFFEE CAKE

CHOCOLATE PECAN & PRALINE COOKIES
**113**

CLEAN CHOCOLATE
**117**

**125**
BROWNIES

STRAWBERRY RHUBARB PIE
**135**

PUMPKIN BUNDT CAKE WITH COCONUT CREAM GLAZE
**147**

COCONUT RASPBERRY "CHEESECAKE"
**151**

**159**
COOKIE DOUGH BALLS

FUDGY PALEO POPS
**167**

Walk down the "Nutrition and Diet" aisle of your local bookstore, or perhaps more likely, browse Amazon.com, and what do you see? There are options for "plant-based," "low-carb," and "fast" (as in "fasting" as well as "fast results"). There are countless celebrities, and celebrity doctors, each endorsing their own particular method, as well as diets based on "superfoods," those based on avoiding foods and even diets for "world peace."

Behind each glossy cover are testimonials and stories, studies and assurances that this diet is "The One." The One diet promises to get you results where other diets have failed. The One tells you that its surefire methods will transform your body easily and effortlessly. The One says that it will make you lean, sexy, and happy. But if every diet claims to be The One, then which One is the right One?

# The Paleo Diet

Unlike every other diet out there, the Paleo diet is the only dietary plan that regards humans from an ecological (evolutionary) perspective. Take, for example, a lion prowling the African savannah, a gorilla in the mist, or an orca swimming in the Arctic seas. Any fifth grader can tell you that lions eat meat, gorillas eat leaves, and orcas eat fish (and seals, but we usually don't tell kids that). Evolution has equipped each of them for the specific task of finding, eating, and digesting their prey, be that prey of the animal or plant variety. So why would humans be any different? In other words, what is our "wild" diet?

Having spent the majority of our time on Earth hunting and gathering the African savannah, we would have had access to animals and plants for eating, as well as water for drinking. There were no processed foods, energy bars, protein shakes, or supplements. There were no supersized sodas or supermarkets. The only fast food was food that ran fast. The only utensils were your hands, and the kitchen looked more like a campsite than a Cuisinart showroom. We survived without modern medical care in the company of poisonous, infectious, and hungry creatures.

Despite all this, humans were remarkably healthy. The inherent danger of our surroundings meant that many people died, often as young children or infants, but if you managed to make it to adulthood, you would have likely had a relatively long life. While this is difficult to prove via fossils or archeological evidence, scientists can study contemporary hunter-gatherer societies as examples of what early man might have been. Extensive research supports the hypothesis behind the Paleo diet: That eating the foods humans evolved to eat is a logical way to achieve optimal health and avoid disease.

# The Missing Link

The problem with diets is that they're often stricken with an extreme case of myopia. In other words, they are so nearsighted, they don't let you see beyond what is on your plate. Counting calories, tracking points, eliminating foods, or adding "superfoods" might all be effective for managing what you eat, but how do you change how you live?

Here at Paleo Magazine, however, we're "big picture" people. This message is right there in our slogan: "Modern Day Primal Living." Notice we didn't say "Paleo Dieting?" Even though we're obviously big fans of the Paleo way of eating, we also make a big deal of the other aspects of ancestral living.

While we promote lots of good-quality meats, veggies, fruits, nuts, and seeds on your plate, we don't want you to stop there. From time immemorial, humans have come together to hunt, to gather, and to eat. It was around food that the first human communities were formed, but in the midst of our hectic modern lives, we've become disconnected from our food, our families, and our world. The reason why we've devoted this valuable space that could have been used to feature more recipes is because we hope that in learning about the important connections that occur around food you will be inspired to strengthen those connections in your own life.

We're about to go on a journey that will span time and space, looking at the biggest events in human history as well as the smallest. Along the way you will likely find familiar subjects explored in a new light as well as new information that feels like something you've always known. We invite you to read the following pages with an open mind, but also a critical one. If we say something is important, do your due diligence and put the idea into practice, experiment and find out if it is true for you.

## This is Your Paleo Recipe AND Lifestyle Book!

This book is the result of the community that has formed around Paleo. Real readers submitting real recipes made from real food! The concept isn't new, but we hope the delivery is slightly different. Our goal is to make the experience of reading this book something special.

In the following sections, we will explore the importance of shared meals and how they can make you and entire family healthier and happier. We will look at how the simple act of going to the grocery store can change more than just what's on your plate. We will get dirty, digging our hands into the ground and starting gardens big and small. Eventually we will even leave the house and go hunting and gathering, literally! Then when the meal is through, we will laugh, play, and eventually rest so we can do it again another day, living, loving, and eating Paleo for optimal health and happiness.

"I spent much of my childhood on my grandparents' farm. Every meal was a special occasion to come together and give thanks for what we had. We bonded over supper telling stories about the day and laughing. The values I learned there didn't have significant meaning in my life until I became a mother, but now I'm attempting to instill them in my daughter's lives by recreating that environment around our table."

—Kendall Kendrick, NTP, **Primal-Balance.com**

The ringing of the dinner bell, the clamoring of kids as they squirm into their seats, the aromas of freshly prepared food. The family table has long been a place to gather for nutrition as well as conversation, connection, and a good old-fashioned argument or two. Memories of family dinners may be fond or not so fond, but they are stereotypical in one way: Only a few generations ago, everyone can remember having one or more shared meals per day. Yet in the span of a single lifetime, the concept of everyone sitting down at the table for dinner has almost become quaint. So why does this matter?

Family dinners satisfy more than a Rockwellian fantasy. There is strong research showing that children who eat a large percentage of meals at home are less likely to participate in risky behaviors. Parents who sit down to eat with their kids are less stressed, and dining in simultaneously fattens your wallet while slimming your waist. Yet despite the multitude of benefits, we are eating together less and less.

To understand the full suite of reasons why family meals are so important and how shared dinners ended up on the endangered species list, we have to go way back, to the first family that could be called human. The reason the qualifier "human" is necessary is due to the fact that, when compared to other animals, we are a peculiar species of social creatures. If we were "lone hunters" like certain species of big cats, perhaps it wouldn't matter if we ate together or not. Many animals are quite happy eating apart from their family; in fact, they much prefer it! To really understand human behavior, however, we should look most closely at the animals separated from us by only a few strands of DNA, the great apes.

## An Ape at the Table

If you were to observe a group of chimpanzees, arguably our closest animal cousins, you would notice some distinct differences between how they share food and how we share food. Mother chimps nurse their young, but beyond that, when it's time to eat, adults don't sit down and wait respectfully for the plate to be passed around. If a chimp were to set out a banquet of fruits, grubs, and monkey meat (a real treat if you're a chimp), it would quickly be stolen and secreted away by other members of the group. Gorillas, too, are solitary eaters. Males are fiercely territorial and will not suffer other silver-backed guys eyeing their harem, but even so, their diet of green shoots and leaves does not lend itself to sharing.

Sharing food presents a paradox. The one doing the sharing seems to get the short end of the stick. Finding food is often difficult in the wild, as perennial superabundance is rare (unless you are a human in a grocery store, which is far from a "natural" environment), so the one doing the sharing seemingly trades a benefit for itself, for the benefit of another. How can this be if evolution is based on the law of "survival of the fittest"? Evolutionary biologists have long studied this question and have several theories that might explain why a given individual would choose to share food, as opposed to simply tolerating its theft.

One theory called reciprocal altruism suggests that humans developed food sharing as a way for the individual to insure him or herself against starvation. Sharing food when you had it was a way to build "social credit." Perhaps today you have enough gazelle meat to go around, but what about tomorrow? If you can't store the food, and assuming you live outside of the Arctic and can't freeze it, it's quite likely to go to waste. Many animals address this issue by simply gorging themselves. Alligators and crocodiles swallow whole deer, never thinking to break off a leg for their neighbor. But they can then go an entire year without eating again. Human stomach capacity, although quite shocking at times (have you ever watched the Nathan's Famous Hot Dog Eating Championships?), is limited compared to that of a crocodilian, so by sharing food rather than keeping it to yourself, you might have the favor returned in kind.

This type of system isn't entirely foolproof, as any school-aged child can tell you. There are "moochers" out there, and in the scientific literature, they are actually called "freeloaders." A freeloader is someone who takes advantage of the generosity of others, but, like a parasite, gives nothing in return. It is possible that many cultural norms, ones that exist in all human societies, are generated to address the freeloader problem. Ideas of "fairness" are deeply rooted and perhaps even innate. Young children will quickly call foul when something "isn't fair."

It could be that we had to share simply to survive. If you look at modern human hunter groups, our clearest example for our prehistoric hunter-gatherer ancestors, you will see that the success rates for hunting are quite low. Although equipped with technology that our ancestors only developed relatively recently, like bows and arrows, modern hunter-gatherers often come home empty-handed. If this even remotely holds true for our ancient ancestors, the lone human hunter would have quickly starved. On the flip side, when the hunter is successful, he typically acquires enough food to feed many individuals, far more than he himself can consume without spoilage (remember there are no refrigerators in the wild!). This excess food provides an opportunity to the hunter, as he can divide it up amongst the community and engender favor among others who desire the prized meat, thus setting the stage for reciprocal altruism.

In observations of modern hunter-gatherers, we can see that the sharing of food is serious business. When survival hangs in the balance, it is a delicate question as to who gets and how much. In an article titled "Hunter-Gatherers and the Mythology of the Market," John Gowdy gives an example of how this event takes place among the modern hunter-gatherer people commonly known as Bushmen:

"Distribution of meat among the Ju/'hoansi is a serious social event. Great care must be taken that the distribution is done exactly right...'Distribution is done with great care, according to a set of rules, arranging and rearranging the pieces for up to an hour so that each recipient will get the right proportion. Successful distributions are remembered with pleasure for weeks afterwards, while improper meat distributions can be the cause of bitter wrangling among close relatives.' By contrast, the market system, by basing distribution on the isolated productivity of each individual, denies the social nature of production and at the same time fragments the social bonds that help hold other societies together."

Reciprocal altruism would explain why we share food, but it doesn't give us insight into the question of who gets what in any given group. Do you give your food to your friends? Your whole nuclear family? Just your wife? Your kids? Where reciprocal altruism drops off, kin selection picks up. Kin selection refers to the idea that we consciously or subconsciously do things to benefit those who share our genes. This is a slightly uncomfortable notion, that we are not fully aware of our motives and that our "genes," these invisible little packets of genetic code, are making decisions for us. But nonetheless, we see kin selection playing out on a daily basis. Who would you expect your parents to provide for, you or your cousins? If you're a parent, would you first help your sister's child or a stranger's?

We'd like to think that we're evolved enough to look beyond such primal notions, but on a practical level, we do what benefits our genes. In prehistoric times, the hunter who acquired large stockpiles of meat and distributed it generously to his closest family members ensured that his genes were passed on. Eventually, genes for behaving in a way that favored one's closest kin became widespread. When a gene takes over, it is considered to be "fixed" in a given species, and so when we eventually spread out across the globe, we took our kin-selecting genes with us. Evolution has some nifty tricks for getting us to go along with the genetic program.

Until the last century, no one knew why having sex worked. Of course, people had been procreating since, well, we began procreating, but it wasn't until the invention of microscopes, and the enterprising soul who decided to look at a particular sort of bodily fluid under a microscope, that the actual mechanics were worked out. Putting the birds and the bees aside, the point is that our understanding of a particular biological process isn't necessary for the process to work. For our genes, it's a relatively simple matter to get us motivated; for anything really, it just has to feel good. In other words, that "warm and fuzzy" feeling you get when you do something advantageous to your genes is nature's way of motivating you to do more good for them. It's like a biochemical "attaboy!" that keeps us on the right track.

If you've ever used Facebook or Instagram, you've seen that people love posting pictures of their food, especially delicious or extravagant meals they've prepared or purchased. In scientific terms, this is referred to as "costly signaling," and it is a way for us to show off and gain social status among our groups. The "costly" part of costly signaling means that whatever it is that is being displayed, the "signaling" part, took a significant investment of time and energy. What was true then is true now. Spending an inordinate amount of time making something truly special when one should really be focused on the practical requirements of staying alive, means that you have energy to burn and resources to spend. In other words, you've got it, and other people should want it.

Costly signaling plays out in other species, too. Take, for example, the peacock's tail. It's a cumbersome thing that makes important attributes like flying difficult. However, being able to grow a large, attractive and symmetrical tail impresses peahens because it displays good genes and ample resources.

For the ancient hunter-gatherer, costly signaling meant investing a huge amount of time learning the difficult skills of tracking and hunting. It also meant spending many days unproductively, coming back empty-handed—until, finally, the hunter bags the big one. Like your uncle's fishing stories, an impressive kill meant years of storytelling and bragging. A hunter could weave yarns that spanned decades. The epic fight to the death where he alone emerged victorious, would grow only more impressive with each retelling. The hunter's wife, initially impressed, eventually tires of his braggadocio, but by then, it was too late; they already had two kids and a mortgage.

## The First Primal Chefs

So far, we've been looking at the hunter half of the hunter-gatherer equation, but in all of these theories, reciprocal altruism, kin selection, and costly signaling, we could give examples for the gatherer as well. When the hunter came up empty-handed, somebody had to be supporting him. In modern hunter-gatherer societies, and likely in our prehistoric past, it is the sharing of food by the gatherer, typically the hunter's wife, that keeps him alive to hunt another day.

The gatherer also provides daily sustenance for her family, supporting her own self as well as many others day in and day out. She does not show off, but through her labor, the family survives another day in the wild. The hunter would do well to say thank you from time to time—flowers would be nice, too.

But how does the gatherer do it? As we've already seen, our close cousins, the gorillas and chimpanzees, don't share food. A mama chimp simply can't feed her family while also feeding herself and a freeloading husband. The fundamental difference between us and them is what we eat, a variable that likely plays into how we eat.

Unlike gorillas and chimps, early humans evolved in a savannah environment that lacked dense forests. We may have even developed a penchant for bipedalism as a result of traversing long distances by foot to find food, losing our climbing skills simply because there wasn't much to need to climb. It is understood that we made our way eating animals like antelopes as well as tubers of various sorts. Eating the animals was simple enough. The hunter either scavenged the kill of another predator such as a lion, or went about trying to kill something directly, sometimes successfully and sometimes not. Raw meat, marrow, and organs were immediately edible, but tubers can't be eaten raw; they have to be cooked. This implies that the ability to control fire occurred simultaneous to our ability to exploit starchy tubers and that this may have been a key step in the development of the human food sharing system. But why are starchy tubers important?

While it might be a vegan fantasy, grass and leaves, the favored items in a gorilla's diet, would scarcely sustain a human. Unlike gorillas, we lack the large fermentative guts that turn plant cellulose (i.e., "fiber") into usable calories in the form of free fatty acids. Ripe fruit, the favorite food of chimpanzees, would have been scarce in the human ancestral environment, making it an unlikely candidate for filling out our ancestral menu. Nuts and seeds are rich in calories and have been known to sustain human populations; the modern hunter-gatherer group known as the !Kung survive by eating large amounts of mongongo nuts in their particular swath of land, but anthropological evidence does not suggest that there was a perpetual superabundant supply of nuts and seeds sufficient to support the original human family.

What we do see, in both modern hunter-gatherers and by virtue of the ecological clues, is that starchy tubers were a key survival food for ancient humans. Abundant in our ancestral environment but relatively useless raw, we would have to first harness fire in order to transform roots into the sort of digestible calories we require. Harvard primatologist Richard Wrangham discusses this in detail in his book *Catching Fire*. In it, Wrangham outlines how the controlled use of fire, which possibly dates as far back as 1,000,000 years ago, was the critical turning point for humanity. Fire warded off nocturnal predators that may have been attracted to a ground-dwelling ape, fire provided warmth that made cold savannah nights bearable, and perhaps most importantly, fire allowed early humans to cook enough food to survive as gatherers when hunting alone didn't suffice.

As modern humans, we are constantly cooking food directly or eating food cooked by others. It is part and parcel to our daily life, so much so that we rarely think about it. However, the implications of a cooked diet should not be underestimated. As we discussed before, food sharing is unusual in the animal kingdom and our closest cousins, the great apes, spend much of their day simply foraging and chewing food for themselves. In other words, usable calories are difficult to come by in nature and surviving on a raw food only diet is very demanding. Harnessing fire, however, changes this equation. Foods that are potentially toxic or indigestible when raw can be transformed into rich sources of calories when cooked. Roots and tubers in particular have this quality and the discovery of cooking them had huge implications for our ancient ancestors and continues to influence us to this day.

With a controlled fire and a days worth of gathered roots, a single person could cook enough food to feed many people. This caloric surplus allowed for other group members to engage in activities such as hunting. This separation of activities, that of hunting and that of gathering, established the first division of labor among human groups and created a subsistence strategy that has served us for 90% of our time here on Earth. With hunting and gathering came the human family as we know it today. A family that survived by working together, a family bound by interdependence, a family that cooked.

The hunter-gatherer lifestyle defined the human experience for hundreds of thousands of years, and along with it, the shared family and community meal. The family unit was interdependent, with each person playing a vital role in bringing something to the table, even if the table hadn't been invented yet. The hunter-gatherer model would allow humans to survive. Adapting their strategy to varying degrees based on local ecology, humans expanded their home range beyond the ancestral land of Africa and spread out across the globe. We became human in body and mind during this time, but, as you well know, a tremendous change occurred at a time known as the Agricultural Revolution.

## Dinner and the Three Revolutions

When the first agriculturalists emerged approximately 10,000 years ago in the Fertile Crescent, the area between the Tigris and Euphrates rivers (in what is now Iraq), humans were ushered into a new age of food production. From the Fertile Crescent came the first domesticated cereal grains, as well as the first domesticated animals. Agriculture changed humans' relationship to food, as we were no longer as dependent on the bounty of Mother Nature. We had, through the use of technology, hacked the ecological system, allowing a smaller number of people to produce greater quantities of food.

Since fewer individuals in a given population were required to participate in food production, agriculture led to a degree of stratification in human society never seen in the more egalitarian world of hunter-gatherers. While there were certainly tribal leaders, both for war and matters of the spirit, in the time following the Agricultural Revolution we saw the first kings, armies, organized religions, and dedicated classes of merchants and craftsmen. Yet, even with all these sweeping changes, the family meal persisted.

In medieval Europe, breakfast was a light meal served first thing in the morning and at what we would consider lunchtime. In the middle of the day, what we would now call lunch was served as the largest repast of the day and called dinner. A smaller evening meal called supper was eaten before bedtime. Supper consisted typically of cold leftovers. These mealtimes were relatively standard until the Victorian era, when cultural norms shifted in response to the first stages of the Industrial Revolution. The stereotypically large "English Breakfast" became stylish during this time, and artificial lighting allowed for dinners to be served later. Among the upper classes, late dinners were considered fashionable, and a means of further separating the wealthy from those bound by the demands of daily labor.

The population transition from rural farmlands to cities during the Industrial Revolution meant that standard meal times continued to change, shifting closer to what is now common in America. In the United States at that time, however, Americans were still largely an agricultural people and the country hadn't been industrialized to the same extent as Europe. As a result, the tradition of a large midday dinner persisted in America into the 1900s. By the 1960s, however, the contemporary custom of a morning breakfast, a midday lunch, and an evening dinner had became commonplace.

As with the Agricultural Revolution, the Industrial Revolution didn't change the basic fact that the family meal was shared with one's family. It is only in the past few decades with the advent of the Technological Revolution that the core of the family meal, and family life itself, has been threatened. The cultural changes brought on by fast food, the microwave, and television set the stage for the demise of the family meal. The impact of personal computers, smart phones, and social media has further eroded this fragile institution.

In the book *Fast Food Nation*, journalist Eric Schlosser describes how the 1950s highway-building binge laid the framework for the nascent fast food industry. With the interstate highway system in place, early fast-food purveyors such as McDonald's provided quick service and low prices, and revolutionized how America eats. Restaurants had existed long before fast food, but with fast food came sophisticated advertising strategies that encouraged consumers to dine out more often. Breakfast, lunch, and dinner could be had on the cheap thanks to never-before-seen economies of scale.

There were other changes in the American culinary landscape in the 1950s. The gas and electric oven ranges that had been longtime kitchen stalwarts found new competition in the form of microwave ovens. Microwaves drastically reduced the time needed to cook a meal, and their adoption was quickly followed by a steady stream of frozen food products tailored to the new technology.

Frozen "TV" dinners, popularized by Swanson & Sons, came pre-cooked and only required reheating. TV dinners had existed prior to the invention of the microwave, but preparing a frozen dinner in the oven took nearly half an hour, compared to just minutes in the microwave. The family meal could now be prepared much more quickly and easily. The need to cook together diminished, as did the need to wait. TV dinners, an oval compartmentalized aluminum tray, were actually named for their TV-like shape, and encouraged consumers to eat in front of their new television sets, no less!

The television was the final innovation of the mid-20th century that struck at the core of the family meal. In the living room, where family games, music making, and reading once took place, the TV quickly came to reign. The black-and-white, and then color, and then 1080p images projected by a cathode-ray tube captured people's attentions like nothing before or since, and TVs continue to become more technologically advanced. There are now 115.6 million homes in the United States with TVs, exposing 294 million people to thousands of channels of programming.

For decades now, television has dominated the entertainment landscape. Starting in the 1950s and '60s, armed with TV dinners balanced on flimsy portable trays, American families gathered around a screen instead of a table. While this was a far cry from our primitive past, this era still favored the family to a certain degree. Although each person may have been eating something different, little energy was expended in the preparation of the meal, and no one even knew where their food came from, yet the family was still technically eating together in a shared experience. All eyes were on the same screen, and it was possible to discuss and debate what was being watched. This would soon change as yet another tectonic shift was looming right over the horizon.

The promise of technology is always that it will make our lives simpler, easier, and more convenient, ostensibly so that we have more time to do the things we want to do, such as spend more time with our friends and families. Yet this promise has proven time and again to be nothing more than false hope. Within a few decades, the Technological Revolution has seen personal computers move from the den, to our laptops, and now, into our pockets. The internet has given us access to an endless supply of entertainment and information, an all-you-can-eat, 24/7/365 buffet of cat videos and *Call of Duty*. Instead of giving us more time, technology has consumed our time, and we are now always plugged in and "on."

Unlike the television, mobile devices offer a personalized experience and an individual screen for just one user. This customized experience is exactly why smart phones have become so popular, and it is also why they are so effective at cutting us off from our surroundings—even from the people sitting across the table. Technology that is always on also means that we are always working. Emails that would have waited in our inbox are now answered immediately and at all times of the day. Few people would imagine calling someone at three in the morning, but receiving and answering text messages in the middle of the night is considered normal. The constant presence of mobile technology means that even when we are together, we are alone in our personal world of likes and dislikes, Facebook friends and email boxes; infinitely connected but completely disconnected.

Technology has also changed the type of work that most Americans do, and this has also had implications for the family meal. For the past century, the traditionally large proportion of the United States' population that lived and worked on farms has been rapidly shrinking, a fact described by economist Joseph Stiglitz, in describing what he calls "the long slump."

"At the beginning of the Depression, more than a fifth of all Americans worked on farms. Between 1929 and 1932, these people saw their incomes cut by somewhere between one-third and two-thirds, compounding problems that farmers had faced for years. Agriculture had been a victim of its own success. In 1900, it took a large portion of the U.S. population to produce enough food for the country as a whole. Then came a revolution in agriculture that would gain pace throughout the century — better seeds, better fertilizer, better farming practices, along with widespread mechanization. Today, two percent of Americans produce more food than we can consume."

Farm jobs weren't easy, but they were predictable in their rhythms. When the work of the day was done, it was done. You could only milk the cows when they needed milking. You could only plant the seeds when they needed sowing. You could only harvest when the crops were ripened. The farmer, living and working on the same land, could come home for dinner in the middle of the day (remember our earlier discussion of mealtimes?), go back to work for a few more hours, and return for supper in the evening. After supper, there would be time for the family to share in the day's events until it was time for bed.

Even the manufacturing jobs that displaced farm work were routine and predictable. When you punched your time card, you could comfortably assume that you were done working for the day. At that time in our history, a shared family dinner could be expected every night of the week, and dining outside of the home was a rare occasion saved for special circumstances. But manufacturing jobs have been on a 50-year slide, as the economics of a connected global economy have shifted the manufacturing base of the U.S. overseas. So what has replaced the agricultural and manufacturing jobs that previously employed most Americans?

According to statistics compiled by the Bureau of Labor Statistics in 2012, the largest occupational groups are now office and administrative support, sales and related, and food preparation and serving related, with approximately 16 percent, 10 percent, and eight percent of the population working in these areas respectively. Annual wages for these occupations average $34,410, $37,990, and $21,380. The largest single occupations are retail salespersons, cashiers, and combined food preparation and serving workers, including fast food, with 3.3 percent, 2.5 percent, and 2.3 percent of the overall workforce employed in these occupations. These jobs have an annual mean wage of $25,310, $20,370, and $18,720. These numbers represent a huge shift in the American labor force and show how physical work has been replaced by customer service and intellectual labor. Additionally, and critically, these jobs seem to be insufficient for most people to pay their bills.

According to a report titled "State of Debt Ranking," CareOne Services Inc., a national debt relief firm, notes that the average household carries more than $10,000 in debt. In a press release, Jenny Realo, a CareOne executive VP, gives an explanation for this debt: "In the last few years, we have seen financial necessity cause more people to turn to credit cards to pay for daily expenses such as groceries, gas and utilities." This debt is in spite of the fact that in 2002, only seven percent of all U.S. married couples were single-income households. In other words, both parents are working, and it still isn't enough to keep most people above water.

Stretched for time and for money, more and more people are turning away from dining at home. Fast food drive-throughs, fast-casual restaurants, and frozen meals are the norm. Even when everyone is at home, busy schedules, television shows, and smart phones keep us occupied and cut off from each other. As explored earlier, dining together as a family unit has been a human tradition since our origins as savannah-dwelling apes. Like the foods we eat and how much we move, our social environment greatly influences our well-being. By missing out on family meals, we suffer consequences that are just as dire as any other disease of civilization.

"Often times we'd feel forced into feeding the boys first and only eating after they went to bed. Rather than succumb to this time wasting fate, we chose to go on this Paleo mission as a family. We now all have one dinner together as often as possible and allow no substitutions. Not only that, but often times, we invite our boys into the kitchen with us to help make our meals so that they feel involved in their own food. This has made all the difference in the world. Now meal time isn't a stressor at all. It's a fun family project that we take on together. It has made our children better eaters. Since they only eat what we eat, they are forced to try new things, some of which they love! It has also added to our feeling of togetherness. We spend meal times talking about all the things we did today from the mundane "Mommy and Daddy posted a recipe on our blog today! Yay!" to the exciting "We went to the zoo today and got to see the octopus eat shrimp! Just like we are!"

—Stacy Toth of **Paleo Parents**,
author of *Eat Like a Dinosaur* and *Beyond Bacon*

The current landscape of life and work in America is that of both parents working relatively sedentary jobs, struggling to make ends meet, and with free time dominated by technology that keeps us apart even when we are together. Food is "quick" and "convenient" but of low quality. Combined, these forces have decimated the traditional family meal. In a Huffington Post article titled "How Eating at Home Can Save Your Life," Dr. Mark Hyman starts with this striking assessment of where we are today:

"The slow insidious displacement of home cooked and communally shared family meals by the industrial food system has fattened our nation and weakened our family ties. In 1900, two percent of meals were eaten outside the home. In 2010, 50 percent were eaten away from home, and one in five breakfasts is from McDonald's. Most family meals happen about three times a week, last less than 20 minutes, and are spent watching television or texting while each family member eats a different microwaved 'food.' More meals are eaten in the minivan than the kitchen."

Dr. Hyman goes on to cite statistics from a study conducted by the Center for Addiction and Substance Abuse (CASA) at Columbia University that looked at the connection between eating at home and the incidence of drug and alcohol abuse among teenagers. The results of the CASA study are startling and emphasize the importance of dining together as a family.

# No to Drugs, Yes to Dinner

CASA interviewed over 1,000 teens and 829 parents, and found that teens who rarely eat at home (defined as fewer than three meals per week) were twice as likely to use tobacco and alcohol, and one and a half times likelier to use marijuana. The top reasons given by teens in the CASA study for why family meals weren't a priority were "at work/late shifts" and "too busy/different activities." For parents, the top reported reasons for not eating together were "too busy/different activities," "don't know," and "at work/late shifts."

The fact that 25 percent of parents reported "don't know" when asked about the absence of family meals, and only two percent of teens said the same, points to an awareness gap among adults. Sixty percent of teens said that they would like to have dinner with their parents more often, a statistic that might seem surprising considering how teenagers are often stereotyped as the ones who want to be left alone. 72 percent of teens reported that eating dinner frequently with parents was "very important" or "fairly important."

So why are family meals important? Earlier we looked at the first human families and saw that it was food that brought families together in the first place. Our physical, social, mental, and emotional systems developed in the context of a close-knit kin group that always shared meals. Looking at it from a more conventional perspective, the CASA study reported that the "magic" of family meals isn't the food itself, but "the conversations around it." Teens reported talking to their parents about what was going on in their lives over dinner, and it was these conversations that strengthened communication and connections between parent and child. While the CASA study didn't look at the relationship between adult couples without children, it is reasonable to expect a similar bonding effect, regardless of the particular family dynamics.

Teens who eat dinner with their families also report that they are willing to become involved in the family meal. Whether it is cleaning dishes, deciding what to eat, setting the table, or preparing the food, these activities create powerful bonds as they unite the family in a shared purpose. Perhaps by connecting with their family in these ways, teens who frequently eat dinner have a safety valve for dealing with the pressures of growing up in a difficult and challenging world, which shows in their improved academic performance and decreased drug and alcohol abuse. If this is not compelling enough, there is still more evidence that supports the positive effects of family meals.

## Fitter Families Dine Together

In a 2011 study published in the *Official Journal of the American Academy of Pediatrics*, researchers performed a meta-analysis of 17 studies that "examined overweight and obese, food consumption and eating patterns, and disordered eating." The researchers found that children and adolescents who have three or more family meals per week are "more likely to be in a normal weight range and have healthier dietary and eating patterns than those who share fewer than three family meals together. In addition, they are less likely to engage in disordered eating." Their results suggest that family meals are a "protective factor" for shielding kids from many nutritional issues.

Although the researchers acknowledged that empirical testing needed to be done to determine the exact mechanisms as to why family meals are protective, they put forth the following explanation:

"It is not surprising that eating family dinners together is inversely associated with eating ready-made dinners, which feature lower nutrient values. For children or adolescents with disordered eating, mealtimes may provide a setting in which parents can recognize early signs and take steps to prevent detrimental patterns from turning into full-blown eating disorders. Indeed, dieting has been recognized as a precursor for the development of eating disorders. In addition, family meals are predictive of family-connectedness, which may encourage adolescents to talk about such issues within their families."

As with the CASA study, family "connectedness" and conversation arise as integral to the family meal as do similar barriers such as "parent work schedules," "difficulty in planning ahead," and "dealing with picky eaters." The meta-analysis also confirmed that kids prefer that their parents "prepare healthy meals at home." Finally, the researchers identified children's and teens' "receptivity in participating in family mealtimes, eating healthy foods, and learning about nutrition."

You may be wondering if the family meal is really necessary if "quality time" is the important factor. Couldn't you just go hang out with your kids at the park? This exact question was researched in a study titled "Correlations Between Family Meals and Psychosocial Well-being Among Adolescents," published in *JAMA Pediatrics* in 2004. The researchers looked at the family meal in particular by controlling for "family connectedness," "parents' marital status," "grade," "race," and "sex," and found compelling evidence for the particular benefit of sharing food.

Study participants, who ranged in age from 11 to 18, were asked specific questions to assess the frequency of shared meals. For example, "During the past 7 days, how many times did all or most of your family living in your house eat a meal together?" The variable of family connectedness was explored with questions like "How much do your feel your [mother, father] cares about you?" and "Do you feel you can talk to your [mother, father] about your problems?" Questions were asked about grades in school, as well as whether or not the child had used cigarettes, alcohol, or marijuana. They also administered a self-esteem questionnaire and used a seven-item scale to determine if depressive symptoms were present. The mental-health component inquired whether the child had suicidal thoughts or had made suicide attempts.

The researchers' findings validated the role of a family meal as more than just family bonding time:

"Frequency of family meals was inversely associated with tobacco, alcohol, and marijuana use; low grade point average; depressive symptoms; and suicide involvement, particularly among adolescent girls. These associations held even after controlling for family connectedness, suggesting that eating meals as a family has benefits for young people above and beyond their general sense of connection to family members."

It is also worth noting that the researchers commented on some of the social and cultural factors that may be preventing more families from having regular shared meals. They proposed "changes in policy" like "requiring after-school activities to end by 6 pm" or a shift away from the cultural expectation of "9-to-5 workers in some sectors to consistently work late" since these present barriers to getting everyone around the table to eat at the same time. They warned, however, that these factors do not absolve parents' responsibility, stating that while there are sometimes extenuating circumstances, oftentimes "the lack of family mealtime reflects priority given to other optional activities."

# The Displacement of Dinner

When the Bureau of Labor Statistics looked at how Americans spent their leisure time, they found that among persons over the age of 15, the average American has approximately five hours of "free time" per day. This is an average across an entire week, so you can imagine that there is typically more free time on the weekends than during weekdays, but nevertheless, these numbers show how we typically spend free time when we have it.

The greatest amount of free time, 2.8 hours, is spent watching TV. "Socializing and communicating" comes in a distant second with 37 minutes. Playing computer games or surfing the internet typically takes up 26 minutes, and "playing sports, exercise, recreation," reading, and "other" activities each take up 18 minutes. We spend the least amount of time per day, 17 minutes, "relaxing and thinking." Perhaps if we did spend more time thinking, we wouldn't watch so much TV!

These numbers clearly support the conclusion that, while large-scale cultural forces such as work schedules and after-school activities make spending quality time with our families a challenge, we are also choosing to spend our time unwisely. In the ancestral health community, discussion of "evolutionary mismatches" often centers on diet and activity patterns; namely, that we eat addictive but nutritionally deficient foods in combination with sedentary lifestyles. However, it is very possible that television viewing also presents an evolutionary mismatch.

Many people follow TV shows religiously, relating to the characters as if they were friends or family members. Through the medium of television, we have a safe way to feel emotionally connected to other human beings without the messiness of reality. The characters in a TV show, whether good, bad, or somewhere in the middle, exist at a comfortable distance, not so close to actually cause harm, but close enough to create the sensation of connection. In a way, we could call these "low-nutrition relationships." How do we increase the "nutritional value" of our relationships? For one, we can invest time in having quality family meals. Many of us are likely out of practice, but it's never too late to get started!

# Clear the Table

So what is the first step? Most people think that you have to commit to a goal, in this case having dinner together as a family for an extended period of time. While some researchers debate the optimal number of days to form a habit from 21 to 90, maybe it's not that complex. According to B.J. Fogg, PhD, Director of the Persuasive Tech Lab at Stanford University, you don't need much time at all. Fogg has been studying the science behind motivation for 15 years and has worked with social media companies like Instagram, specializing in getting people to sign up for and participate in their services. But he has now turned his attention to something smaller—something tiny, in fact. His new project, Tiny Habits, encourages people to take tiny steps toward their desired change.

Actually, Fogg thinks the first thing you need to do is have an epiphany. Epiphanies don't often come easily, but hopefully the previous material in this chapter has given you a starting point. Let's assume you've seen the proverbial light and are planning to make a change. Now that we've got that out of the way, you might be thinking of a laundry list of things to do, schedules that need to be changed, groceries that need to be bought. If you're feeling overwhelmed, take comfort in the fact that this is exactly how a normal person would feel.

## Coming back to the present, what would be the very first step in getting a family meal onto the table?

If you're like the average American, your kitchen table has become a repository for a great many things: mail, newspapers, laundry, computers, and perhaps a sleeping cat or two. Fogg thinks that creating the proper environment is second only in importance to having an epiphany, so what sort of environment does a cluttered kitchen table create? Certainly not one conducive to a family meal. Step one, then, is to simply clear the table. Not make dinner, not buy groceries, just clear the table. Whatever is trash goes in the trash, whatever needs to be sorted gets sorted, and—sorry, Fluffy—no cats allowed.

Now that the table itself has been reclaimed, turn your attention to the room itself. What does the area surrounding the table look like? Has the clutter from the table simply shifted to the floor? Assess the area and look for ways to beautify and brighten it. A simple centerpiece of flowers and a few candles is an obvious choice, but perhaps you could set the mood in other ways. Consider how restaurants lull you into their establishments. They play music, they hang pictures of beautiful foods, and they remind you wherever you go that this is a place to relax, eat, laugh, and have fun. Take a page from their playbook and do the same by making your home your "favorite restaurant." If this is all sounding a little too artsy-fartsy, don't fret: There is sound science to support the importance of setting the right mood.

# Don't Stress—Digest

In his classic treatise on stress, *Why Zebras Don't Get Ulcers*, Stanford University biology professor Robert Sapolsky paints the following picture. Imagine an animal (let's say a zebra). The zebra is grazing on grass in a wide plain, when its ears perk up suddenly. It has heard a suspicious rustle, and with wide flaring nostrils has caught the scent of its eternal foe, the lion. The lion bursts out of the bush and the zebra takes off. A heated chase ensues. Both animals push their bodies to the utmost limits, but with a well-timed juke, the zebra manages to outmaneuver the lion and breaks away. Several minutes later, with the lion at a safe distance, the exhausted zebra lies down in a shaded paddock and takes a well-deserved nap.

Now imagine the typical day for your average American. On the roadway, with one hand on the wheel and another clenching a sugar-laden energy drink, our specimen nervously scans the traffic ahead. Pulling a long swallow of fluorescent green liquid from the can, he thinks about how late he is for work and what excuse might allow him to keep his job for another day. An opening emerges between a semi-truck and a Humvee and he pulls out, slamming his foot down on the accelerator, heaving his Honda Civic into the gap. The semi-truck driver blasts his horn and flips the bird, causing the car driver to wheel around and yell back, spilling his energy drink. Traffic once again grinds to a halt, and now the frazzled motorist flails around the front seat, trying to find a napkin to dab his now day-glo pants. Unsuccessful, he sits and stews, grabbing a candy bar from his bag, angrily tearing away the wrapper and absentmindedly chewing the half-melted confection as he daydreams of creative ways to get revenge on the idiot truck driver.

What do these two scenarios have in common? What is different? In both situations, the autonomic nervous system of all the participants is stimulated. This part of our nervous system is so called because it is automatic, with responses triggered by deep reflexes outside of our conscious control. It is also divided into two halves, each with a distinct role. To generalize, the job of one half is "fight or flight," while the other's role is to "rest and digest."

In the zebra, the sympathetic or "fight or flight" branch was stimulated when it sensed the lion. This branch prepared the zebra's body for activity that would allow it to escape from harm. The lion's attack represents what is referred to as an acute stress, one that occurs at a high intensity but intermittently. In the example of the driver, however, the sympathetic branch was stimulated by being late to work, by drinking caffeinated beverages, and by having a near-accident with a truck driver. This is what we would call a chronic stress, one that occurs at a lower intensity but is repetitive and unrelenting. Another major difference, and one that we will cover later, is that the zebra used the stress response to power its activity. The driver, on the other hand, remained sedentary despite being awash in stress hormones.

The second part of the zebra's story is also critical, and it is the one that has the most relevance to our discussion of the family meal. After an intense bout of life-saving exercise, the zebra laid down and took a break. In doing so, the zebra's parasympathetic or "rest and digest" branch was stimulated. This allowed the zebra's body to send blood back to the digestive system so it could assimilate nutrients from the food that was being digested. The car driver, whose parasympathetic nervous system never had an opportunity to activate, didn't digest his food properly, setting the stage for disease in the long term and misery in the short term. Activation of the parasympathetic "rest and digest" branch of your autonomic nervous system is necessary to set the right mood when you sit down to eat!

As if this weren't enough, rushing around in a constant state of anxiety and scarfing your meals down when you're stressed doesn't just mess with your digestion. It also messes with your head, and it might even be making you fat! In a 2000 University College London Department of Epidemiology and Public Health study called "Stress and Food Choice," researchers found that "stressed emotional eaters ate more sweet high-fat foods and a more energy-dense meal than unstressed and non-emotional eaters." Although the exact mechanisms haven't been discovered, it is likely that stress increases appetite. Researchers theorize that stress used to mean that you had to do some sort of physical work, like running away from a lion. It is only in recent history that the human creature has been confronted by the cocktail of chronic stress, unlimited access to food, and a sedentary lifestyle. This unholy trinity is a trigger for our current obesity and diabetes epidemics, as well as a host of autoimmune diseases.

Some people might be inclined to think that trying to sit down to eat as a family is simply going to add to stress levels, but research from Brigham Young University (BYU) that was published in the June 2008 issue of *Family and Consumer Sciences Research Journal* suggests just the opposite. This study found that sharing a family meal actually reduced job-related stress in both fathers and mothers, although the effect was more pronounced in moms. A press release from BYU that discussed the findings noted: "Normally the level of perceived work-family conflict directly increases with each hour worked. In this study, work-family conflict remained the same for women working up to 60 hours a week, so long as work did not interfere with dinnertime." In other words, even with a stressful job, coming home to a family meal serves as a positive counterbalance to the stress of modern life.

If you arrive home for dinner and are still feeling stressed, take a long, slow, deep breath. This age-old advice not only clears your head, but it increases activation of your parasympathetic nervous system, helping you to relax and unwind. In a 2006 paper titled "Physiology of long pranayamic breathing: neural respiratory elements may provide a mechanism that explains how slow deep breathing shifts the autonomic nervous system," researchers at the Augusta Women's center hypothesized that "voluntary slow deep breathing functionally resets the autonomic nervous system through stretch-induced inhibitory signals and hyperpolarization currents propagated through both neural and non-neural tissue which synchronizes neural elements in the heart, lungs, limbic system and cortex." That's a doozy of a sentence, but the main point is clear: A slow, deep breath puts the breaks on the stress cycle and may be a great exercise for you and your family to do together before eating dinner.

Now that a nice, relaxed setting for your family meal is in place, the natural question arises of what to eat. As someone interested in the Paleo lifestyle, you've probably been introduced to a wide range of foods that would be considered "weird" in normal circles. According to CDC surveys, "33 percent of adults meet the recommendation for fruit consumption and 27 percent get the recommended servings of vegetables," so even a diet high in fruits and vegetables, let alone one that features organ meats, bone broth, and fermented foods, is outside of the mainstream. Children especially are notoriously picky eaters and can be the bane of many well-intentioned meal plans, but what if being a fussy eater is actually "Paleo?"

## The Perplexing Plight of Picky Eaters

While infants are happy to eat just about anything, bugs and buttons included, toddlers and young children are often hesitant to try new foods. This reluctance to eating novel food items is called neophobia, which translates to "fear of new things or experiences." In an attempt to understand this behavior, scientists at the Cancer Research UK Health Behaviour Unit at the University College London gave detailed questionnaires to 564 mothers to look for patterns in rejected peas and pushed-away carrots. Their findings suggested that being a picky eater likely made very good sense in our ancestral past.

The lead researcher of the study, Lucy Cooke, interpreted the data as follows:

"Plant toxins can be very dangerous to children, as could the effects of food poisoning from unrefrigerated meat. So it makes sense that humans may have evolved to be highly suspicious of certain food types as youngsters, and only to trust foods they have eaten before. The problem is that strategies which were sensible for children to adopt thousands of years ago are not such a good idea now, and may be contributing to the low levels of vegetable and fruit consumption in the British population generally. Understanding the evolutionary basis for our children's eating habits is very important, because it will allow the development of strategies to get children eating healthily. For instance, if children see their parents eating a particular food before having to face it themselves, they may be reassured that it is unlikely to do them any harm."

Leafy vegetables, meats, and fruit, all healthy parts of a modern Paleo diet, were the foods most likely to carry a risk of toxicity or food poisoning for children in the Paleolithic era. Perhaps not surprisingly, then, these foods were found to be eaten in the least quantities by modern picky eaters. On the other hand, consumption of "potatoes, cereals, biscuits, crisps, and cakes" was "normal." In case you are wondering, "crisps" are potato chips, and the fact that kids, even picky ones, tend to eat them with abandon, may even be connected to the fact that starchy tubers have always been cooked, even in the Paleolithic, which reduces their likelihood of being toxic or transmitting a foodborne disease.

This doesn't mean you should throw in the towel on serving up a healthy family meal, but it does mean that you are going to have to employ some strategies to overcome your children's natural Paleolithic tendencies. A good way to do this is by giving your children multiple exposures to a food before expecting them to buy into eating it. In a 2003 study in the *European Journal of Clinical Nutrition*, researchers offered children various foods over the course of eight days. They asked the children to rate how much they liked the food (in this case, pieces of sweet red pepper), and then asked them the same question at the end of the study. At the study's end, the children rated the pepper more highly, and they were also eating more of it. A separate group of kids was bribed with stickers as rewards if they ate the pepper, but this strategy proved to be less effective than that of gradual and consistent exposure. These findings suggest that you can make one family meal, rather than taking individual orders, and expect your kids to eat it as long as you give them some time to warm up to the idea of foods like kale, collard greens, or spinach.

Sitting around the table together is also a great way to talk to kids about the deeper benefits of food, giving them insight into where it comes from, how it grows, and what it does for their bodies. Even adults can benefit from this type of talk, assuming that they are open to it. The opaque modern industrialized food system benefits from the fact that we know so little about what it puts into our food and where the ingredients come from. The conversation doesn't have to be forced, but can emerge as a natural result of engaging with the preparation of the food itself. When appropriate, have your family take part in the cleaning, cutting, or cooking of vegetables. Maybe cook up a whole chicken or carve a primal cut of beef with your kids. Take advantage of your child's natural curiosity and give them food for thought as well as nutrition for their bodies.

Food marketers target kids with images that give the message that their food is "fun," making home-cooked meals seem boring by comparison. Try taking a page out of this playbook and apply these techniques to healthy options. Preparing the food so that it can be eaten by hand, arranging it to look like animals or faces, or just making sure that it actually tastes good can go a long way toward enhancing the experience for your children. Nutritional therapy practitioner Kendall Kendrick recommends throwing an "indoor picnic" by simply eating dinner on the floor.

## Skipping Takeout Saves Money

If your spouse or significant other is the sticking point keeping you and your family from sitting down to eat, perhaps a discussion of the economics of eating in can provide the necessary motivation. In the 2007 Consumer Expenditure Survey from the Bureau of Labor Statistics, it was found that the average household spent $4,465 on meals at home versus $2,668 on meals eaten outside the home. At first glance, this seems to contradict the idea that eating at home is cheaper, but when you look at the numbers on a per-meal basis, you'll see the picture change.

Since 30 percent of meals are typically eaten outside the home, the annual expenditure for dining out breaks down to an average of $8 per meal. The per-meal cost of a meal eaten at home, however, averages a much lower $4.50. These cost savings are realized because you are essentially buying your food in bulk when you go to the grocery store and cutting out the middleman, the restaurant. You are also taking on the added responsibility of preparing the meal. Rather than looking at this role as a burden, you could look at it as a sacrifice in the truest sense of the word.

## Make Sacrifices for Your Family

Sacrifice literally means "to make sacred," and that's what you're doing when you take the time to prepare and share in a family meal. This time, free of TV, cell phones, and other unnecessary distractions, truly becomes sacred since it gives us a rare moment of intentional and authentic experience. This can be emphasized with the creation of rituals or the reintegration of old traditions. Saying grace or even a few words of thanks can create a touchstone that calls attention to the importance of food, family, and the value of life itself.

Family meals might be on the decline, but you have the power to buck this trend. The health of you and your family is too important to be given up for the sake of short-term convenience and comfort. The road might not always be smooth, and kids won't always eat their Brussels sprouts, but keep coming back to the table, night after night. Maybe put some bacon on those Brussels, and in time, dinnertime, and your family, will thrive.

For more information about getting your family meal on track, visit **www.TheFamilyDinnerProject.org**

We know that the family meal and the complex social interactions that it fosters are integral to our health and wellbeing. Our relationships are strengthened by the conversations and connections forged at mealtimes. The time and energy invested by sharing a meal with loved ones pays huge dividends in terms of physical, emotional, and social health. Unless you are engaged in a little hunting and gathering of your own (a subject we will cover in a later chapter), the food that makes up your family meals comes by virtue of someone else's labor. But who are these "someone elses" who produce our food? What would happen if, like in our own family unit, we turned our attention to strengthening the relationships we have with those who grow, harvest, and transport our food?

Unfortunately, however, most of us participate in a food-production system that distances us from the realities of the field and the farm. The farmers, ranchers, and growers whose hands are in the soil and on the tractor wheel are nameless and faceless to the typical consumer. We might be able to imagine what farming looks like, but these images are often just a composite of what we've seen on TV. The truth is, we often have no idea where our food comes from, let alone who is growing it. This distance between the production of food and the consumption of it is in some cases unintentional, a simple byproduct of an increasingly globalized society. National boundaries have become more permeable and, as the laws of economics and profitability dictate, goods and services will seek the path of least resistance. In other words, the cheapest method of production wins the day, and if this means shipping food from faraway lands, then so be it. However, globalization alone can't explain the reason for our collective farm-to-plate disconnect.

The methods and means of modern food production are the domain of a handful of large-scale food producers. These companies generate huge profits by exploiting animal, plant, human, financial, political, and natural resources. By their way of thinking, sustainability, animal welfare, and the production of healthy food for consumers are barriers that stand in the way of quarterly earnings and shareholder obligations. Corners are cut at every turn, and conditions at many food-production facilities (it would be wrong to call them "farms") are so disgusting that food companies actively prevent consumers from knowing what is going on behind the scenes. These operations, vast monocultures of grain or confined animal feeding operations (CAFOs), operate with profitability as their only motivating ethic, leaving it to future generations to pick up the pieces left in their wake. If we were to see or smell their impacts firsthand, it would likely turn our stomachs and close our wallets. Yet as consumers, we instinctively want to know, and to trust, the people who produce our food. How then, is this sleight of hand accomplished?

The way big food producers fill the trust gap and give us a sense of confidence and connection is through a sophisticated system of manipulation and propaganda otherwise known as "marketing." They create brands and products that "speak" to us as if they were friendly neighbors or friends. They examine our wants and our needs, fulfilling them with sparkling packages and catchy phrases. They wage these campaigns over the airwaves, through the television, and on the internet. There is no escaping the constant barrage of targeted marketing that constantly says "trust me," and once they have their hooks in, it is simply a matter of cultivating that "brand loyalty" over a lifetime.

Yet we are not purchasing these products directly from the manufacturers. We aren't visiting their fields, their CAFOs, their factories, and their warehouses. If we were, we would actually have a relationship with them. We would see the workers, the crops, and the animals, and we would likely want to talk with the management. We would have a conversation with them about why things are done the way they are. The producers of the food would also see us. If we arrived at their door with our prescriptions, our obesity, our diabetes, and our lost loved ones, they would at least see the impact of their efforts. Perhaps they would be motivated to change. Instead, they keep us at arm's length by allowing middlemen to push their products. It is essential to understand how these middlemen came to be if we want to know how our relationship with food producers fell apart.

## The Story of Supermarkets

Supermarkets are so ubiquitous that they hardly stand out from the fabric of our daily experience. Rushing through our shopping trips, we hardly think about the supermarket itself, too busy throwing items into our carts, lulled into a stupor by muzak and the aroma of freshly baked bread. The store, however, is intimately aware of you. Informed by science and psychology, its seemingly innocent layout represents a deliberate effort to extract as much money as possible from every customer. Once you step across the supermarket's threshold, you become a target. Each of the 15,000 to 60,000 items, known in industry terms as "stock keeping units" or "SKUs," has been strategically placed for the highest possible return on investment. Eye-level candy and sweet cereal for kids, bathrooms in the back of the store that force you to walk past the bakery, "loss leaders" designed to draw you in: This hasn't always been the case, however, as the supermarkets of today are a relatively recent invention, one that revolutionized the way we consume food.

The first store that we could call a supermarket was opened in 1916 by Clarence Saunders. Located in Memphis, Tennessee, Saunders' Piggly Wiggly store introduced the shopping public to checkout stands, individually priced items, and standardized product locations. Piggly Wiggly did away with the grocery store clerks who traditionally took and filled orders from customers. Instead, Piggly Wiggly patrons were encouraged to make their way through a maze of departments filled with edible goods and individually select the products they wanted to purchase.

By displacing the grocer with the consumer, the supermarket system created an increased need for attractive packaging and name-brand recognition in order to appeal to customers. Early marketers used print ads and the burgeoning media of radio to target specific demographics. Whether it was "convenience" for busy moms, "fun" cartoons for kids, or "manly" products for Dad, effective marketers instinctively knew how to push their customers' buttons. In the half-century since, these efforts have become increasingly refined, utilizing the latest technology to peer into shoppers' brains. The field of "neuromarketing" uses technology like magnetic resonance imaging (MRI) to make observations of "the shopping brain" to decipher the way we make buying decisions, to inform how to hack our shopping circuits and create even more-irresistible ads.

Another difference between supermarkets and traditional grocers was in the way they generated profits. Piggly Wiggly and its successors focused on selling massive quantities of goods, pricing them more cheaply and turning products over more quickly. Rather than storing large amounts of inventory and selling each item at the highest possible price, supermarkets made a small profit on a large number of items. This new business model led to a new focus on lower prices and encouraged large chain supermarkets to bypass food wholesalers, purchasing their products directly from the manufacturer instead. Much like Wal-Marts do today, this allowed supermarkets to outcompete the small independent grocers who depended on selling smaller quantities of higher-margin products.

Supermarkets also capitalized on the emergence of refrigerated shipping and food storage. Prior to the widespread availability of refrigeration, on both the retail and consumer level, people had to shop for their food daily. Most items were purchased fresh, and typically from a neighborhood market. Bakers offered bread products, butchers offered meats, and produce vendors specialized in one or more types of fresh fruits and vegetables. Grocery stores traditionally focused on dried goods that were either imported or difficult to produce at home. Items like sugar, salt, coffee, tea, tobacco, and spices were common items found at grocery stores prior to refrigerated shipping, but the ability to transport fresh foods to locations far away from the field, orchard, or fishery allowed them to expand their offerings even further.

The shifting distribution of the American population also worked in supermarkets' favor. Prior to World War II, much of the population was concentrated in major urban centers such as New York and Chicago, but after the war, an urban diaspora emerged as vast numbers of people moved into the suburbs. These new population centers created a demand for products and services, and supermarkets were ideally positioned to take advantage of this demand.

The supermarket revolution created a new focus on product marketing that emphasized the selling of large quantities of cheaply priced goods. It offered one-stop shopping that did away with the specialized grocers of yesteryear. Supermarkets also made fresh foods available year round, giving us tomatoes in the winter, lamb in the fall, and corn, wheat, and soy in just about everything all the time. The previously de facto practice of "seasonal eating" faded away, and the personal connection we once had to food producers faded with it. Our interactions are now conceptual and abstract rather than authentic. A brand, logo, or marketing campaign designed by scientists may be compelling, but it is superficial and one sided.

# Earl Butz, the Birth of Big Food and How Corn Became King

Supermarkets are responsible for much of the distance between us and our food, but if we continue to peel back the layers, we find that the means of food production bear little resemblance to the old-fashioned homesteads we envision when we think of farms. A handful of multinational corporations, referred to collectively as Big Food, manufacture much of what is found in the grocery store, and consequently, much of what we eat.

The agribusiness monopoly consists of companies like ConAgra, Archer Daniels Midland, and Monsanto that have managed to subvert the sensibility and the senses of the food-consuming public. In Marion Nestle's 2002 book *Food Politics: How the Food Industry Influences Nutrition and Health,* Nestle documents a laundry list of Big Food misdeeds that are only now receiving widespread public attention. Whether it is aggressive lobbying of politicians, the employment of paid experts who advocate for false health claims, or the use of deceptive marketing tactics, Big Food has made tremendous profits by playing politics.

In many ways, the story of Big Food is similar to that of supermarkets, with increased centralization, decreased variation, and technological innovation playing key roles. There is also a visionary in each of these stories, a single person to whom much responsibility can be attributed. In the case of supermarkets, it was Clarence Saunders; for Big Food, this person was Earl "Rusty" Butz, secretary of the United States Department of Agriculture (USDA) under Richard Nixon.

At the time Butz came into office, agricultural policies reflected the legacy of the Great Depression, a legacy that sought to prevent the ecological destruction and economic hardship that swept through the Midwest during the Depression-era Dust Bowl. The Dust Bowl was an ecological disaster that swept across the Midwestern United States in the 1930s. A combination of weather patterns and human intervention set the stage for a widespread loss of topsoil in the form of vast clouds of dust. The human role in this event was the removal of native plains grasses and the planting of cereal crops. Farmers, accustomed to the agricultural practices that had worked on the East Coast, didn't realize that the favorable precipitation that seemed to "follow the plow" in the Great Plains was transient. Unaware that drought conditions would soon return, they plowed up the native grasses in the quest to plant more and more crops.

When arid conditions did eventually return, the lack of native grasses left the soil vulnerable to erosion. Eventually, hot winds ripped across the plains and vast clouds of dust formed, literally blowing the land, and the farming communities that depended on the productivity of the land, away. The term "Dust Bowl" was coined by an AP reporter named Robert Geiger, who used it to describe the devastation wrought upon states like Oklahoma, Arkansas, Missouri, Iowa, Nebraska, Kansas, Texas, Colorado, and New Mexico. What followed was an unprecedented mass migration of Midwestern farmers, and many years of difficult recovery.

In *The Grapes of Wrath*, a fictionalized account of one family's experience trying to escape the ecological and personal tragedy of the Dust Bowl, American novelist John Steinbeck wrote:

"And then the dispossessed were drawn west—from Kansas, Oklahoma, Texas, New Mexico; from Nevada and Arkansas, families, tribes, dusted out, tractored out. Car-loads, caravans, homeless and hungry; twenty thousand and fifty thousand and a hundred thousand and two hundred thousand. They streamed over the mountains, hungry and restless—restless as ants, scurrying to find work to do—to lift, to push, to pull, to pick, to cut—anything, any burden to bear, for food. The kids are hungry. We got no place to live. Like ants scurrying for work, for food, and most of all for land."

With images of the Dust Bowl lingering in the public imagination, the Roosevelt administration was able to implement policies that sought to discourage the agricultural practices that contributed to soil erosion. As part of the New Deal, Roosevelt included widespread management efforts that supported crop diversity, measures to conserve water and soil resources, and insurance programs for farmers whose livelihoods often depended on fickle weather patterns. The government also created a system in which they would sometimes pay farmers to let their land go unplanted as a means to stabilize crop prices and ensure both a living wage for farmers and reasonable prices for consumers.

If a surplus on the market threatened a price collapse, the government would issue payments to farmers, who would then allow their fields to go fallow. This would gradually eliminate the surplus, causing prices to rise. On the other hand, if prices got too high and started hurting consumers, the payments would end, crops would be planted, and supply would once again increase, which would lower prices. To Butz, however, these policies were obstacles to production, efficiency, and the spirit of capitalism, useless friction that stood in the way of a new American farm that would "feed the world."

A series of events that saw food prices climbing put Butz in an advantageous position to do away with the New Deal farm policies. Public concern emboldened executive action, and in a June 1973 address, President Nixon proclaimed that "there is one great problem that rightly concerns every one of us, and that is, as you know, rising prices, and especially rising food prices." The reason for rising prices, he states, included "increased demand at home and abroad, by crop failures abroad, and as many people in various areas of the country know, by some of the worst weather for crops and livestock that we have ever experienced." Nixon concluded that "the time has come to take strong and effective action" to deal with the problem of rising food prices. This was the thinking that provided Butz with his mandate to recreate the American agricultural landscape, to see fields planted "from fencerow to fencerow" and to maximize rather than to manage production.

Butz convinced farmers that foreign trade, specifically US grain sales overseas, would keep prices high, avoiding a supply glut and price collapse. He provided proof of his concept by organizing a massive grain sale to the Soviets who, at the time, were in dire need of food imports. Domestic crop production in the Soviet Union was faltering, and they eagerly bought up American grain, clearing out US surpluses and providing an economic boon to farmers. "It was like a tremendous burden had been lifted," noted one farmer who remembered Earl Butz after his death in 2008. "We were finally making money, and we had a champion who was watching out for us. He made us proud to be producing food for the world."

The changes in agricultural policies instituted by Butz were initially welcomed by farmers, partly because farms had long been subsistence operations. Profit was often secondary to the day-to-day demands of feeding a family. In an interview for the Southern Oral History Program Collection, farmer Lauch Faircloth summed up the situation:

"The first goal of agriculture was to subsist. If you could pick up any change, a little money on something, [that was] well and good, but the first role of agriculture was for the landowner and the workers to subsist. I grew up in that economy. People were just absolutely everywhere going into 1939. I've forgotten the percentages, but you can check them. It was like thirty percent of the people were unemployed. If you went to underemployment, over fifty [percent] had no job. Massive amounts of them were [working] on subsistence agricultural operations. We called them farms. They were there because they could produce a little corn, a few hogs, keep a cow, and survive. That's what agriculture was. [You'd] can a lot of beans in the summertime and go through the winter. Money was practically an unknown and a very, very rare item at best."

The technological and societal changes brought about by World War II also played a role in Butz's agricultural revolution. Farm workers had been increasingly deserting the fields for factories as the wartime manufacturing boom promised high wages and steady work. After the war was over, the machinery of war continued to power the American economy, and farm workers stayed at the factory. With fewer hands to tend the fields, farmers turned increasingly to technology to make up in efficiency what they lacked in manpower.

The arduous tasks of plowing and harvesting were typically done by hand, assisted by pack animals like mules. Gasoline-powered tractors and combines allowed a single person to do the work of many men and animals. Surplus munitions also found their way to the field in the form of the first widely used chemical fertilizers. Ammonium nitrate, a chemical used to make explosives, had been synthesized many years before by scientists who discovered that nitrogen and hydrogen gases could be turned into solid compounds under high heat and pressure. Again, fossil fuels were key as the heat required for this reaction could only be achieved through the use of fuels like oil, coal, or natural gas. When applied to crops, however, the raw ammonium nitrate becomes what we call fertilizer, as it provides usable nitrogen to plants.

In nature, nitrogen comes from soil bacteria that convert or fix atmospheric nitrogen. The family of plants called legumes, which include grasses like clover and alfalfa, as well as peanuts, soybeans, and lentils, have specialized structures in their roots that contain these nitrogen-fixing bacteria. However, with the advent of nitrogen fertilizers, soil fertility could be controlled and production increased at will. Crop rotation and the occasional fallow period became a thing of the past as a single crop could now be planted year after year. Single-crop agriculture, known as monoculture, had arrived, and with it, a certain species of grass emerged as the king of crops. Not all plants respond well to chemical fertilizers, but one plant in particular has a seemingly insatiable appetite for it. This plant is a grass species native to South America known scientifically as "zea mays" but more commonly as corn.

Corn was the ideal crop for Butz's new vision of American agriculture. With the mantra "Get big or get out," Butz urged farmers to increase the size of their farms by buying more land, to upgrade their machinery, and to plant more corn. Loans were needed to finance this expansion, and, when the agricultural bubble eventually burst, this translated into vast amounts of unpayable debt. The companies that would eventually become today's Big Food moved in and bought up the farms, consolidating their holdings on the seeds, land, and fertilizers and pesticides that were now needed to be competitive in the global grain marketplace.

Butz's legacy is the seen on the supermarket shelf, where a full quarter of the items stocked are actually corn in some form or another. Corn is in the drinks, the meat, and even the floors and walls. In an article titled "What's Eating America," food writer Michael Pollan explains:

"For the great edifice of variety and choice that is an American supermarket rests on a remarkably narrow biological foundation: corn. It's not merely the feed that the steers and the chickens and the pigs and the turkeys ate; it's not just the source of the flour and the oil and the leavenings, the glycerides and coloring in the processed foods; it's not just sweetening the soft drinks or lending a shine to the magazine cover over by the checkout. The supermarket itself—the wallboard and joint compound, the linoleum and fiberglass and adhesives out of which the building itself has been built—is in no small measure a manifestation of corn.

While we can thank Butz for the fact that our grain-based foods are cheap, the average American spends less on food than anyone else—six percent of our annual income on average. We can also thank Butz for rising healthcare costs, environmental costs, and reliance on limited fossil-fuel resources. Additionally, direct subsidies to agribusiness continue unabated. Butz himself said in an interview that "[a]nyone who believes we're going to stop direct payments to farmers in 2002 also believes in the tooth fairy," and he was right.

Between 1995 and 2012, commodity subsidies, of which corn tops the list, cost US taxpayers $177.6 billion, with only 10 percent of farms collecting 75 percent of that amount. When these costs are taken into account, it becomes clear that "cheap" food is actually quite expensive. Commenting on this situation, Karen Pendergrass, author of *Eat Paleo—Save the World*, warns that "[t]he more centralization we get, the more taxpayers pay in subsidies. We never hear about the environmental disasters that occur at agricultural sites, but taxpayer dollars go to clean it up. So not only do we pay them upfront in subsidies, we pay to clean up after them, we pay for their "cheap" food, and then pay for our health care costs. Buying CAFO meat is like shopping yourself out of health and a better economy." It may seem like we have found ourselves in a hopeless situation, a trap for which there is no escape. Yet there is hope amidst the bleak industrial food landscape.

## Local, Slow, and Paleo

If we are to repair our relationship with food producers, we must be willing to take a hard look at our own role in the producer-consumer disconnect. We have to ask: Are we happy to buy cheap industrial food? Should we ignore our gut sense that something is amiss, hoping that the problem will solve itself or that someone else will do it for us?

Becoming part of the solution starts with knowledge and awareness, as the character Morpheus explains to Neo in the movie *The Matrix*: "This is your last chance. After this, there is no turning back. You take the blue pill: The story ends, you wake up in your bed and believe whatever you want to believe. You take the red pill: You stay in Wonderland, and I show you how deep the rabbit hole goes." Knowledge is the "red pill." It is what opens the door to a new understanding of how the world works and your place in it. By reading books such as this one, it is safe to assume that you have already taken the red pill. The next step is taking action, but where to start? It may seem like there is no escaping supermarkets and Big Food, but the truth is that we are not alone in our fight. A burgeoning grassroots effort is aimed at attacking the problem from both ends.

On the production side, an increasing number of farmers have become tired of participating in the industrial food system. Squeezed by contracts that favor the "value" added by processing food into food products, they receive a smaller and smaller percentage of every dollar's worth of the food they produce. The "get big or get out" approach encouraged farmers to make up for diminished profits per pound by producing more, taking a volume approach similar to that of the supermarkets, but this has proven to be a futile task given that farmers shoulder all of the liability incumbent in food production. This arrangement leaves farmers constantly on the brink, deeply indebted, and often working additional jobs just to make ends meet. For farmers who wish to maintain their livelihood, their livestock, and their lifestyle, the growing demand for better-quality food has emboldened them to start thinking small again.

Compared to the vast monoculture operations that currently dominate food production, there are several benefits to operating a smaller, more diverse farm. Referred to as polycultures, these operations mimic natural systems by utilizing biological diversity to limit the need for chemical pesticides, herbicides, and fertilizers. The variety of animals and plants that can be produced also reduces the farmer's dependence on the success of only one crop. If weather conditions fluctuate, as they always do, conditions for corn, or wheat, or soybeans may be unfavorable, leading to disaster. In a polyculture, however, there is always another option. To use financial terms, this represents a more diversified portfolio, and what is good for the financier is good for the farmer.

Size also works to the small farmers' advantage. The average farm today is 441 acres, and the average age of the principal operator is a little over 55. To manage a farm of this size requires expensive machinery, and even satellite mapping. All of this technology is expensive to purchase and maintain, and regular updates are needed to ensure that the farm stays competitive. Contrast this to a small operation, typically ranging from 1 to 20 acres, where crops can still be harvested by hand, animals pull the plow, and animal "waste" is used for fertilizer. The reduced overhead and operating expense of a small farm translates into less debt and dependence. If there is one thing that small farms are dependent on, it is you, the consumer, having access to their products.

There are several ways to bring farmers and consumers together, the most elegant of which is to buy your food directly from the farm. This puts the most money back into the farm and supports its continued operation. Of course, this only works if consumers are able to efficiently find farms in the first place, but fortunately this is an area where technology has dramatically leveled the playing field. In the past, farmers wishing to sell their products directly would be limited to setting up signs or a roadside stand, or running ads in the local paper. While this would bring in a small number of patrons, it's inadequate to fund a viable business. With the growth of the internet, however, consumers can easily find local food producers by searching websites like www.Localharvest.org or www.Slowfoodusa.org.

From a personal and ecological health perspective, direct farm buying also helps consumers to actually see how their food is produced, effectively closing the gap that has been widening since the advent of industrial agriculture. For people following the Paleo diet, this means having direct knowledge of the feed used to raise animals, reducing dependence on confusing labels that claim "grass-fed" but leave out "grain-finished." This also allows you to observe the health and living conditions of the animals, again eliminating the need to decipher the differences between "cage free" and "free range."

When it isn't possible to visit farms directly, the next best option is to buy semi-direct, whether through a farmers market or Community Supported Agriculture (CSA). In 2012, there were 7,864 farmers markets listed in USDA's National Farmers Market Directory, representing a 9.6 percent increase in 2011 alone. Farmers markets allow consumers the convenience of predictable hours and a centralized location for purchasing a variety of goods that might not all be available at an individual farm. Farmers markets also provide the opportunity for face-to-face interaction between farmers and consumers, who can get to know their food producers and ask questions about their operations.

CSAs are often available at farmers markets, but they offer a different sort of relationship and operate based on the purchase of full or partial farm "shares." With the purchase of a CSA share, consumers receive part of what the farm produces based on the season and local conditions. This guarantees income for the farmer, allowing operating expenses to be budgeted for ahead of time and streamlining the farm's marketing efforts. For the consumer, CSAs provide an opportunity to try things that they might never purchase at the store. Never tried kale? Well, now you have five pounds of it, so you'd better start looking up some recipes. This sort of arrangement also has the added benefit of rekindling the relationship that the consumer has to the land. For example, many of us are accustomed to eating bland, tasteless tomatoes that have been picked green, ripened artificially, and shipped thousands of miles. With a CSA, however, you can have great, nutritionally superior fresh tomatoes that actually taste like tomatoes. If you want to eat them year round, you can learn how to can and preserve your food, an activity that provides opportunities for family fun and further connection.

The third option is to continue shopping at grocery stores. Perhaps this means going to a greener store such a Whole Foods. Such stores tend to advertise when food is local, but they conveniently avoiding saying anything about the items they import. In this setting, there is typically more information about growing conditions, for both animal and plant foods, but it is often limited to a label or an informational pamphlet. Trusting such information requires a leap of faith on the part of the consumer and provides an opportunity to cut corners and mislead on the part of the producer. Many so-called "organic" products are still produced by industrial operations that have seen the label as an opportunity to make more money by selling at a premium price. This may represent a marginal improvement in terms of the practices employed, but often it is little more than a marketing gimmick.

Even in the context of a conventional supermarket, if consumers make a commitment to purchasing only whole, unprocessed food, our relationship to food producers would be changed, undermining the entire system of industrial food. In a Gnolls.com blog post titled "Real Food Is Not Fungible: How Commoditization Eliminates Nutrition, Impoverishes Farmers, and Destroys The Earth," J. Stanton describes how much of the "food" we eat is in reality a commodity. He defines a commodity as "a good supplied without qualitative differentiation across a market," and provides an example of how industrial corn fits this definition: "Like most commodities, grains are mixed without regard to source: the producers sell their corn, whereupon it's transferred via an elevator to a silo and mingled with all the other corn from the area, and anyone who buys corn simply gets whatever comes out of the elevator first." Now, contrast this to the hypothetical purchase of real food and how it resists commoditization: "For instance, when we go to buy onions, tomatoes, melons, or other produce, we don't just choose them at random. We choose the variety that will taste best in our recipe, and from that, we choose the ripest, least damaged, best-looking, best-smelling ones available. We may even reject all the choices as unsuitable and visit a different store...or the farmer's market."

Ultimately, for the relationship between food producers and food consumers to heal, both sides have to be willing to reach out. The farmer has to decide whether or not to continue participating in a system that is familiar but untenable and the consumer has to go outside of his or her comfort zone, first buying only whole foods and then striving to source those foods in the most direct manner possible. In the middle of this relationship, there has to be an exchange, of money as well as of information. Trust needs to be built and cultivated. Small local farms are increasing in number, but for them to provide real competition to Big Food, consumers have to be willing to pay more for their food, to be more discriminating, and to go out of their way to find good things to eat.

To find sources of local food in your area, go to **www.EatWild.com**

Picture this: driving to a restaurant, sitting down in a comfortable chair, browsing a menu, and ordering a meal from the wait staff. The food arrives, and the meal is consumed. Conversations are had and connections are made. A short while later the bill arrives, and someone pays. The meal is over, and everyone leaves. The plates are cleared and the process is repeated.

The food served in the above scenario may have been of the utmost quality, local, grass fed, sustainable and organic, prepared impeccably with love and attention. The company dining together may have shunned their smart phones, and partaken in meaningful conversation. Maybe they even talked about the food they ate, considering each bite instead of mindlessly stuffing their faces.

Perhaps instead of a restaurant, the gathering occurred at the home of a friend or family member. The homemade food was served on plates that didn't match, but no one minded because the company was good and the food even better. Everyone helped clean up afterward, and plans were made to "do this again soon." A few stragglers stayed behind, inspiring the host to break out a special bottle of wine saved for just this sort of occasion.

It's hard to imagine anything wrong with either of these examples. Dining at an amazing restaurant or having the ultimate meal with close friends is hard to beat. The experiences are rich and full of deep human connection of the sort we explored in Chapter 2. No dollars were given to the industrial food system, and the relationship between food growers and food consumers was honored and appreciated. Yet there is something missing; there is something disconnected.

In both situations, at the restaurant and at the home, the relationship with the food was just that: "food." It is easy to forget in the midst of our modern experience that the word "food" is an ecological term. As Joel Salatin of Polyface Farms says, "Chicken breasts don't grow on trees," and neither do steaks, pork chops, or fish filets. Apples, oranges, and many other things do in fact grow on trees, but have we climbed those trees to pluck these fruits? Have we watched the flowers bloom, the pollinating of flying insects, and the long maturation that culminates finally, briefly, and ephemerally with a perfectly ripened orb of sweetness and seeds? Do we think of the fruit as something for us rather than something that uses us as a means of propagating the next generation of plants?

And what about the chicken breast, steak, pork chop, and filet? Or, should we say, the chicken, cow, pig, and fish? When we find ourselves in the presence of these creatures, we are more likely to name them things like Betty, Bessie, Babe, or Nemo rather than "food." They are animals, like us, that just so happen to be living at a time when we, emboldened by technology, sit atop the food chain.

The ethics or righteousness of our relationship to animals and plants has been much debated and will continue to be controversial. What is certain, however, is that we are part of a vast exchange of energy that flows across the surface of this planet in a profusion of forms, animal, plant, bacterial, and fungal. The raw materials of life are constantly being traded, shared, and borrowed; the consumer eventually becomes the consumed. Whether this is "right" is secondary to the fact that it "is" and it is a system that we cannot escape.

Modern society, with the creation of neatly packaged "foods" and even more-processed "food products" has made it easy to forget this fact, to simply ignore it. We live in a world in which less than one percent of the population, living behind an opaque curtain of agribusiness interests, feeds the other 99 percent, who blindly eat what they are given.

In an episode of chef Jamie Oliver's television show *Food Revolution*, an example of this blindness was made painfully clear. Oliver showed a group of schoolchildren a tomato, asking them if they knew what it was and where it came from. The kids were unable to identify it, probably because the only tomatoes they eat come in the form of high-fructose-corn-syrup-laden ketchup. This should be shocking, newsworthy material for public debate and impassioned action. Instead, *Food Revolution* was cancelled, replaced by reruns of *Dancing with the Stars*.

As is often the case, the situation looks dire and futile, but inevitably there is a glimmer of hope. We can connect with our food in more meaningful ways. We can get to know food as more than stuff found in brightly colored boxes. We can learn the rhythms of the season, discovering our place in the vast web of life. We only have to be willing to get dirty and go wild.

## Shopping on the Savannah

A group of people sits around a campfire. They are surrounded by a sparse landscape, a vast grassland peppered with the occasional stand of trees. The pitch-black sky is a riot of stars, and the moon is fat, shining brightly despite its pockmarked face. An animal cries out in the darkness, and the members of the group draw closer to the fire, thankful for its warmth and for the safety it offers. They are people as we know people. If it weren't for their animal-skin clothing, painted skin, and bodies adorned with jewelry crafted from bone and shell, you'd be unable to pick them out in a crowd.

Physiologically identical to us in every way, capable of creative thought, language, and the entire suite of skills that define "human," these people were our ancestors, the first branch on our collective family tree. In what is now known as sub-Saharan Africa, they managed to survive by living entirely off the land. When they were hungry, they banded together. Using skills passed down through the generations, they would track and slaughter game animals like antelope, although a bird or lizard would do in a pinch. After a successful hunt, there would be feasting and celebration. But game is unpredictable, and the hunter often returned empty-handed. It was in times like these that the gathering of roots, shoots, and other edible plants sustained the group. Deciphering the puzzle of what is good to eat and what is poisonous, inedible, or just plain bad must have claimed innumerable lives and soured many stomachs, but with trial and error, humans persevered and flourished.

The suite of skills, the sheer amount of knowledge, and the direct experience required by hunter-gatherers just to survive in the wild is nearly incomprehensible. Jared Diamond, author of *Guns, Germs, and Steel*, has proposed that in many ways hunter-gatherers utilized more resourcefulness and creativity than do "civilized" humans. A hunter would have to identify many types of animals, know their sounds and movements, and understand their temperament and their territory. A gatherer would have to know many more varieties of plants, some for food and some for medicine, as well as where to find them and how to prepare them. All of this information would be passed down from generation to generation by story, by song, and by hand as no written language, books, or YouTube would have been available.

For hunter-gatherers, there would have been no doubt whatsoever regarding where their food came from, what it was, or even who killed or harvested it. This intimate knowledge of the plants and animals they ate fostered respect and admiration. Irving Hallowell, who studied the significance of the bear in Arctic hunter-gatherer groups, observed how "animals are believed to have essentially the same sort of animating agency which man possesses. They have a language of their own, can understand what human beings say and do, have forms of tribal or social organization, and live a life which is parallel in other respects to that of human society."

While hunting for one's own food is scarcely necessary in today's world, it might be even more important than ever. The knowledge of and respect for animals that was cultivated in hunter-gatherer society by the daily need to hunt can be cultivated intentionally today. If we are willing to eat a piece of chicken, beef, or pork, but unwilling to see that act for what it is, the death of one living thing for the life of another, we are denying responsibility for our choices. The modern food system, in packaging and processing food into oblivion, takes advantage of this sort of willful ignorance, raising animals in terrible conditions and creating industrial systems for dispatching them, often brutally and painfully. Hunting, on the other hand, brings us into full awareness of what it means to eat meat.

In an article titled "Why hunting your own dinner is an ethical way to eat" on CNN.com's *Eatocracy* blog, journalist Lily Raff McCaulou outlined five reasons why she chooses to hunt for meat as an environmentalist. She cites the light environmental impact of hunting ("no antibiotics, artificial hormones, pesticides, herbicides, or unnatural feeds"), the misery of factory farming ("My venison was never confined, castrated, or branded the way most farmed steers are."), the lack of waste ("After I shoot an animal, I gut and butcher it myself... And I'm confident that as much of the animal as possible is used."), and the conservation efforts funded by hunting licenses ("Proceeds from the Federal Duck Stamp – a required $15 annual purchase for migratory waterfowl hunters – have added more than five million acres to the national wildlife refuge system.") as the rationale for her hunting conversion.

While it might not be practical for everyone to suddenly stop shopping and start shooting their dinner, obtaining a portion of your daily meat from hunted game will certainly impart a new appreciation for food; it might even save you some money. In a blog post by "The Midwest Texan," the actual dollar value of hunted game was meticulously calculated. After accounting generously for equipment, licenses, and other expenses related to hunting, the price per pound of hunted venison worked out to approximately $2.81. This number isn't just for ground venison either; it's for all cuts, steaks, chops, tenderloin, and roasts. The average price per pound of beef (even conventionally raised beef) can't compare to this sort of bargain.

Hunting therefore provides an economical way to source truly natural meats from animals that have eaten a biologically appropriate diet, have lived free of confinement, and were dispatched with a minimum of pain and suffering. To hunt in an appropriate manner, proper training in the use of firearms, licensing, and respect for the animals being hunted is absolutely necessary. Illegal poaching of animals and cruel acts disguised as "hunting" stand in stark contrast to the spirit of hunting for necessity, for food, and for an appreciation of our role in the complex web of life. Hunting isn't limited to animals; foraging, even in urban environments, provides an opportunity to similarly connect with wild plant life.

## Foraging for Food

"I feel this overall sense that we need to reconnect with nature. We've lost that here [largely due to] the evolution of the industrial complex [which] grants validity to the notion that we're only supposed to buy from stores."

—Ethnobotanist Marc Williams of Botanyeveryday.com

The hand of Big Food hasn't touched only commodity foods such as grains, fruits, and vegetables. In a Mark's Daily Apple post titled "On the Problems of Cultivated Fruit," *Primal Blueprint* author Mark Sisson observes that there is something amiss at the produce aisle:

"Besides the strange and overflowing array of boxed or bagged, artificially flavored wonders that fill the aisles in the average grocery store, we've all agreed that there's something else rather "twilight zone"-esque about our forays into the supermarkets. Specifically, has anyone noticed the mammoth size of fruit sold at the grocery store? What's more, this Amazonian "beautiful" fruit just doesn't taste the same, does it?"

Fist-sized strawberries, stereotypically red and glistening, blemish free and, apparently perfectly ripe, yet they taste like... not much. Giant glistening apples that, with the first bite, fail to impress. The same could be said for the bananas, the broccoli, the tomatoes, and the squash. Few of the fruits and vegetables at the grocery store taste the way they should, a fact that makes perfect sense when you consider that they have been produced in a manner that is the vegetable equivalent of CAFO beef.

The produce aisle is dominated by products raised for speedy growth, large size, uniform appearance, and ease of transport—products that, if they aren't technically genetically modified organisms (GMO), are significantly modified for the purposes of profit. Consumers are somewhat culpable in this situation, as we typically prefer to buy aesthetically appealing produce. Unfortunately, this has set up a vicious cycle in which appearance has become the primary factor in determining how produce is produced. As expected, this push for "pretty" foods has come at a price—and in this case it's more accurate to say "prices."

Plants growing in the wild are subject to harsh conditions that include insect predation, drought, and sun exposure. Unlike animals, however, plants cannot defend themselves or move away from harmful environments. Their strategy for survival involves producing a wide range of chemicals that act as natural pesticides, sun blocks, and more. These chemicals, collectively known as phytochemicals, have allowed plants to flourish in some of the most unlikely of circumstances. When a human eats a plant that contains these chemicals, some of them are absorbed into the digestive tract and end up in the blood stream.

We derive health benefits from phytochemicals both directly and indirectly. The direct benefit arises from the ability of antioxidants to bind to disease-causing molecules inside our bodies called reactive oxygen species or "free radicals." This is exactly the role that they perform in plants, which is why it is simply a matter of good fortune on our part that they are healthy for us too. Free radicals are a natural byproduct of cell metabolism, yet they cause damage to our cells, damage that accumulates and manifests as chronic disease. Phytochemicals are also believed to have indirect health effects that come about by the stimulation of mechanisms involved in cell maintenance and DNA repair. How this process works isn't well known, but what it boils down to is that plants can be really good for us to eat.

When plants are grown conventionally, however, the application of artificial pesticides, herbicides, and environmental controls reduces the need for plants to develop natural phytochemical protections of their own. The result is a fruit or a vegetable that is not only less beneficial from a nutritional standpoint, but one that also lacks in the flavor and taste departments. Organic farming methods, especially those techniques that mimic nature, can restore much of the antioxidant potential, and flavor, of foods—but another solution presents itself in the form of foraging.

Foraging is the common term used to describe the practice of going out and finding edible plants and fungi in the wild. From berries and cherries to garlic and greens, wild edibles abound across the country, and they can appear even in unlikely urban environments. Wild plants, like wild game, are truly organic. As a result, they are far richer in nutrition and more intense in flavor than their cultivated counterparts.

While foraging never really went out of style in Europe and in some pockets of the United States, it largely fell out of fashion in this country with the rise of supermarkets and agribusiness. Recently, however, foraging groups have begun popping up in foodie hotbeds like San Francisco, New York, and Portland, Oregon, stimulated in part by the Great Recession of 2008. The trend quickly expanded across the country as people looking for free foods that tasted gourmet took to the forests in what is equal parts shopping trip and treasure hunt. Yet for all of its benefits, foraging does pose certain challenges.

Modern hunter-gatherers, as well as our hunter-gatherer ancestors, possessed living traditions that guided their foraging activities. These traditions not only provided knowledge of which plants were palatable and which were poisonous, but they informed the way that these resources were exploited. Lacking this knowledge, we are at risk of overexploiting wild resources and picking them clean. Miles Irving, a foraging instructor who responded to an article published in *The Guardian* that questioned the wisdom of "new foraging," offered this bit of insight:

"Our present ecological crisis springs from being insulated from our surroundings and the effects of our actions. People should forage, precisely because it can be overdone. Immoderate foraging produces immediate environmental feedback, teaching hunter-gatherer lesson one: if you don't take care of a resource, you lose it."

So whether it's dandelion greens for your salad, a handful of trailside raspberries during your hike through the woods, or a wild asparagus sauté with your steak, foraging for wild edibles can be an enjoyable, healthful, and economical way of reconnecting with the earth and our ancestral food-gathering traditions. That is, of course, assuming that you exercise proper respect for the natural resource, learn how to identify edible plants from a qualified teacher, and don't go foraging on someone else's property without their permission.

## Out of Eden and into the Garden

It is well known that hunting and gathering as a survival strategy defined human existence for most of our time so far on Earth. In the movie *The Search for the Perfect Human Diet*, Dr. Loren Cordain, author of the book *The Paleo Diet*, gives the analogy of a 100-yard football field that represents the entirety of human history. Walking the field from end to end, yard after yard goes by, the equivalent of hundreds of thousands of years, until, at the very end, only the last few inches represent the emergence of agriculture and the Neolithic age.

This analogy draws a clear line between human groups—those who hunted and gathered and those who favored agriculture—but the true story of human development is more complicated. Between Paleolithic hunter-gatherers and Neolithic agricultural societies (referred to as "agrarian") are the horticulturalists, the first gardeners. First emerging approximately 20,000 years ago, horticultural societies lacked the domesticated draft animals of agrarian societies, relying instead on human labor. Their technological toolkit was also more limited as stone and wood implements, rather than metal, were used to dig, cut, and plow. The fruits, roots, vegetables, herbs, and nuts cultivated by horticulturalists required skillful weeding, watering, and fertilizing, but on a much smaller scale than later forms of agriculture. Horticulture also seems to have emerged independently in various human groups.

While we know that agriculture emerged primarily from the Fertile Crescent, new evidence suggests that this wasn't an isolated event. In the Pacific island nation of Papua New Guinea, cultivation of starchy taro roots may have begun as early as 10,000 years ago without any direct contact with people from Asia. On the other side of the Pacific, along the coast of North America, the cultivation of seafood, an early form of aquaculture, may have been in practice. Dana Lepofsky, an archaeologist at Simon Fraser University in Vancouver, combined archaeological findings with local oral history to conclude that native British Columbians deliberately and consciously managed their marine and other food resources, creating clam gardens and fish traps by building rock walls and pools in intertidal zones.

The emergence of horticultural practices in a wide variety of human groups shows that we have long directed our intellectual and creative capability toward the challenge of understanding natural processes. This changes the story from a "this" or "that" model (either a hunter-gatherer or an agriculturalist) to a more nuanced conversation about our relationship to plants and animals. Commenting on this perspective, Katharina Neumann, an archaeobotanist at the Johann Wolfgang Goethe-Universität in Frankfurt, Germany, suggests that "[a]griculture and wild plant exploitation do not exclude each other. More and more scientists think that the development from foraging to farming was gradual and not a rapid revolution."

In the words of Michael Pollan, gardening "suggests there might be a place where we can meet nature halfway," and this statement represents why gardening can play an important role in reconnecting us with our food. Gardens tend to be intimate and personal, and they are cultivated in or around the home. A windowsill herb garden, a backyard row of collard greens or kale, or a compost bin in the kitchen can create a proximity to nature and natural processes. With a garden, death and decay are no longer final; they simply represent a fallow period when the old is tilled under to make way for the new. Waste becomes fertilizer, and is therefore never wasted. The hustle and bustle of daily life is slowed down. Flowers will not be hurried into fruits; they emerge slowly, hesitantly at first, then suddenly take shape and ripen. Food is anticipated for months and weeks, making its appearance in a favorite dish that much more important.

A garden can also become more than a philosophical experiment; it can hold real practical value. During World Wars I and II, "war gardens," sometimes referred to as "victory gardens," were planted on both public and private lands. These gardens were seen as a way to give people at home a way to feel like they'd contributed to the war effort, but they were no mere morale booster. At their peak, victory gardens actually produced upward of 41 percent of the produce consumed nationwide. During the Cold War, the Caribbean nation of

Cuba found itself dependent upon the Soviet Union for imports of petroleum and other goods, but when the Soviet Union collapsed, these imports dried up. Organic urban gardens, known in Cuba as "organoponicos," emerged as a grassroots solution to the crisis, and now nearly 70 percent of the vegetables and herbs grown on the island today are produced by organoponicos.

There is power in producing food, and by planting a simple backyard garden, you are taking that power away from multinational food conglomerates and putting it back into your own hands. A garden is a place to meet nature, but it is also an opportunity for nature to meet you. Any size and any scale is a step in the right direction, whether this takes the form of a simple herb garden or a full-scale homestead. Gardening puts us into a direct relationship with our food, forming a connection that transcends the specific items we are growing. If you have seen a tomato from seed to fruit, you will never be able to look at an industrial tomato the same way. The curse has been lifted, the seal has been broken, and the spell has been withdrawn. Food is no longer a product, a label, a box, or a package. It is a living thing, and in caring for it, we can't help but appreciate it. To understand a thing is to truly love it.

If you want to get dirty and learn how gardening can change the world, watch "Ron Finley: A guerilla gardener in South Central LA" at TED.com

Or, if going wild better suits your style, discover your own foraging forest at **www.FallingFruit.org.**

# PALEO
## MAGAZINE ™
*modern day primal living*

*Recipe page 68*

**BALSAMIC MARINATED
SKIRT STEAK** WITH
PEACH MANGO SALSA
**page 60**

**BEET & MARROW SOUP**
*page 62*

Paleo Garden
Burger **PAGE 80**

**MORNING**
Egg Muffins
page 74

## RECIPES

# Almond
# Butter Bark

Estimated Prep Time: 10 minutes
Estimated Cooking Time: N/A
Serves: 8-10

1/3 cup coconut oil, softened
1/4 cup almond butter
2 Tbsp coconut flakes
2 tsp honey
Sea salt, to taste
Dark chocolate, for shaving

You'll be able to make a thicker bark if the almond butter is cold. If warm, it will spread very easily.
**IF YOU CAN'T DO NUTS, REPLACE THE ALMOND BUTTER WITH SUNFLOWER SEED BUTTER.**

1. Mix coconut oil, almond butter, coconut flakes, and honey in a bowl.
2. Spread on a parchment-paper-lined cookie sheet.
3. Sprinkle with sea salt.
4. Use peeler to shave dark chocolate over the top.
5. Place in freezer for about 1 hour.
6. Enjoy!

As seen online:

# Bacon-y Baba Ghanoush

Estimated Prep Time: 20 minutes
Estimated Cooking Time: 30 minutes (for eggplant)
Servings: 2 cups

1 large eggplant
1/4 cup tahini
2 cloves garlic
Juice of 1 small lemon
1/8 tsp ground cumin
1/2 cup loosely packed Italian parsley
2 Tbsp extra virgin olive oil (plus extra for drizzling)
4 slices bacon
Sea salt, to taste
Pepper, freshly ground, to taste

1. Preheat oven to 375°F.
2. Poke the eggplant all over with a fork and place on a parchment-lined baking sheet.
3. Bake 30 minutes, until very soft. Remove from oven, let cool slightly, then peel off skin and discard.
4. Meanwhile, cook the bacon in a medium skillet until done. Cool, then crumble. Set aside. Reserve 1-2 Tbsp bacon fat.
5. Cut peeled eggplant into large chunks. Place in a food processor or blender.
6. Add tahini, garlic, lemon juice, cumin, salt and pepper, parsley, olive oil, and reserved bacon fat to the food processor. Puree until smooth, about 1 minute.
7. Transfer the mixture to a serving bowl. Stir in most of the bacon crumbles, reserving a few for the top.
8. Drizzle with olive oil, sprinkle with remaining bacon crumbles, and add a sprig of parsley for garnish. Serve at room temperature with cut-up veggies. Refrigerate leftovers for up to 3 days in an airtight container.

As seen in:

# Baked Cinnamon Fennel and Pears

Estimated Prep Time: 10 minutes
Estimated Cooking Time: 20 minutes
Servings: 2

1 large fennel bulb, sliced lengthwise into ¼" pieces, fronds discarded
2 large pears, cored and sliced into ¼" pieces
2 Tbsp extra virgin olive oil
1/4 tsp ground cinnamon
1/4 tsp sea salt
1/4 tsp ground pepper

1. Preheat oven to 350°F.
2. Place fennel and pears on a baking sheet and drizzle with olive oil. Sprinkle with cinnamon, sea salt, and pepper.
3. Bake for 20-25 minutes or until soft.
4. Serve warm or chilled atop salads.

As seen in:

# Balsamic Marinated Skirt Steak with Peach Mango Salsa

Estimated Prep Time: 10 minutes
Estimated Cooking Time: 8 minutes
Servings: 4

**Marinade:**
1-1/2 to 2 lbs grass-fed skirt steak, cut into approximately 8" pieces
3 Tbsp coconut aminos or wheat-free tamari soy sauce
1/4 cup olive oil
3 Tbsp balsamic vinegar
3 garlic cloves, minced
1/4 tsp dried basil
1/4 tsp marjoram
1/2 tsp granulated garlic
1/2 tsp granulated onion
1 Tbsp honey
2 Tbsp tomato paste

1. Place all marinade ingredients in a gallon size resealable plastic bag, seal, and squish the bag around to combine.
2. Place skirt steaks in the bag, seal, and press meat around to cover with the marinade. Refrigerate for 4 hours or overnight.
3. Allow steaks to come to room temperature. Preheat grill to medium-high heat.
4. Grill steaks over hot coals, about 2 minutes per side. Use real hardwood briquettes in a cast iron Lodge BBQ for great, even cooking.
5. Place steaks on a warmed platter, tent with foil, and let rest for 10 minutes.
6. Slice steaks into strips, against the grain and serve with Peach Mango Salsa (see ⟶ ).

As seen in:

## Peach Mango Salsa

1/2 small red onion, diced
1 large peach, diced
1/2 mango, diced
1 small jalapeño, diced, with seeds and ribs removed
1 medium avocado, diced
Juice of 1 lime (about 2 Tbsp)
2 Tbsp olive oil
Sea salt and freshly ground pepper to taste

1. Place all ingredients in a medium bowl and stir gently to combine.
2. Refrigerate until needed. This salsa is great fresh, but is best if made a few hours before using to allow flavors to combine.

**Options:** Add chopped cilantro for another level of flavor! Salsa is also great combined with chicken or pork. And if you like things spicy, leave some of the white ribs on the jalapeño before dicing. If you're really heating things up, leave some of the seeds in too!

# Beet & Marrow Soup

Estimated Prep Time: 20 minutes
Estimated Cooking Time: 60 minutes
Servings: 4

3 lb marrow bones
2 lb beets, peeled and chopped
1 lb carrots, peeled and chopped
3 stalks celery, chopped
1 shallot, minced
2 Tbsp coconut aminos
1/2 tsp rosemary
1/2 tsp tarragon
1/4 tsp turmeric
1 tsp sea salt
Pepper, ground, to taste

1. Preheat oven to 450°F.
2. Roast bones (cut sides up), beets, carrots, and celery in oven for
   25 minutes. Remove and add to stockpot.
3. Add just enough water to pot to cover veggies and bones.
   Add shallots, coconut aminos, rosemary, tarragon, turmeric, salt,
   and pepper. Stir well. Bring to a boil.
4. Reduce heat and simmer for 30 minutes, or until veggies are soft.
5. Remove bones with slotted spoon. Be sure all the marrow falls out
   and remains in the pot.
6. Using an immersion blender, blend until smooth.
7. Serve and enjoy!

As seen in:

# Coconut Chicken Strips

Estimated Prep Time: 15 minutes
Estimated Cooking Time: 20 minutes
Servings: 4

4 organic boneless, skinless chicken breasts, cut into strips
1/4 cup olive oil

**Breading:**
1 cup finely shredded unsweetened coconut
1/4 cup coconut flour
1/2 tsp sea salt
1/2 tsp freshly ground pepper
1/2 tsp granulated onion
1/2 tsp granulated garlic
1/2 tsp paprika

1. In a shallow dish, combine breading ingredients. Set aside.
2. Drizzle olive oil over chicken strips. Dredge strips in breading, covering all of the chicken.
3. Place breaded chicken in a greased 9" x 13" glass baking dish. Bake in a 375°F oven for 20 minutes.
4. Change oven to broil and broil chicken about 5 minutes, or until golden brown on top.

As seen in:

**PALEO**
MODERN DAY PRIMAL LIVING

BACK TO SCHOOL

MAKE TRICK-OR-TREATING LESS SCARY.

HONEY:
Nature's Perfect Sweetener?

# Cranberry Orange Macadamia Scones

Estimated Prep Time: 15 minutes
Estimated Cooking Time: 25 minutes
Servings: 8

**Dry ingredients:**
2 cups roasted, unsalted macadamia nuts
  (if using salted, omit sea salt)
1/3 cup coconut flour, sifted
1 tsp baking soda
1/4 tsp sea salt

**Wet ingredients:**
1/4 cup pure maple syrup
1 tsp pure vanilla extract
2 eggs
1/4 cup melted coconut oil
Juice from 1 organic orange (about 1/3 cup)

**Add-ins:**
1 cup chopped fresh cranberries
Zest from 1 organic orange

As seen in:

*PALEO MAGAZINE*
MODERN DAY PRIMAL LIVING

**Happy Holidays!**

**The Past**
Microbes and Human Health
Agriculture and the Autoimmune
Epidemic

**The Present**
Stay Inspired For Winter Workouts
What Really Matters?

**The Food**
Cranberry Orange Scones
Bacon Baba Ghanoush
Bone Marrow Soup
And More!

1. Preheat oven to 350°F.
2. Place macadamia nuts in a food processor and pulse until a coarse meal forms.
3. Place macadamia meal and remaining dry ingredients in a medium bowl and stir to combine.
4. Add the wet ingredients, except coconut oil, to the macadamia meal mixture and blend with a hand mixer until combined.
5. With mixer on low, slowly pour in the coconut oil. Mix well. Let the batter sit 5 minutes to thicken.
6. Stir in chopped cranberries and orange zest.
7. Using a 1/2-cup scoop, make 8 even balls of dough and place on a parchment-lined baking sheet. Flatten each dough ball slightly with the back of a spoon or the palm of your hand.
8. Bake 21-24 minutes, or until golden brown and the center of the scone is firm to the touch when pressed lightly.
9. Cool on pans for 5 minutes, then move to wire racks to cool completely. Store leftovers in an airtight container up to 3 days or freeze up to 3 months.

# Easy Crab Soup

Estimated Prep Time: 20 minutes
Estimated Cooking Time: 20 minutes
Servings: 6

2 Tbsp extra-virgin olive oil
3 scallions, thinly sliced
10 cherry tomatoes, halved
1 cup vegetable broth
2 Tbsp lime juice, freshly squeezed
2 large carrots, julienne
1/4 cup finely chopped fresh cilantro
1/2 lb lump crab meat
1/4 tsp garlic salt
1 tsp crushed red pepper
1/4 tsp sea salt
1/4 tsp freshly ground pepper
2 tsp slivered almonds
1/4 tsp fresh lemon zest

1. Heat oil in a large saucepan over medium heat and add tomatoes;
   cook for 2 minutes.
2. Add remaining ingredients and cook for 15 minutes. Serve warm.

As seen in:

PALEO
MAGAZINE
modern day primal living

PALEO & RELIGION
Evolution meets religion. How they fit together in the Paleo community.

Jessica Biesiekierski
We chat with this award-winning researcher on the practical implications of FODMAPs.

ADRENAL FATIGUE
WHY YOUR BODY STRESS RESPONSE SYSTEM CAN BECOME CHRONICALLY EXHAUSTED AND WHAT TO DO ABOUT IT.

Business Spotlight
Lava Lake Lamb

# Who Needs a Resolution? Green Smoothie

Estimated Prep Time: 5 minutes
Estimated Cooking Time: N/A
Servings: 4

1 cup cold coconut water or plain water
3 cup loosely packed spinach leaves
2 medium carrots, unpeeled and chopped
1/2 English cucumber, unpeeled and sliced
1 green apple, cored and sliced
Juice of 1 lemon
1/3 cup loosely packed flat leaf parsley
1 stalk celery, chopped
3 ice cubes
2 Tbsp melted coconut oil

1. Add all ingredients except coconut oil to a blender. Blend until smooth.
2. With blender on, slowly drizzle in coconut oil through opening in the lid.
3. Pour into 4 glasses and enjoy!

As seen in:

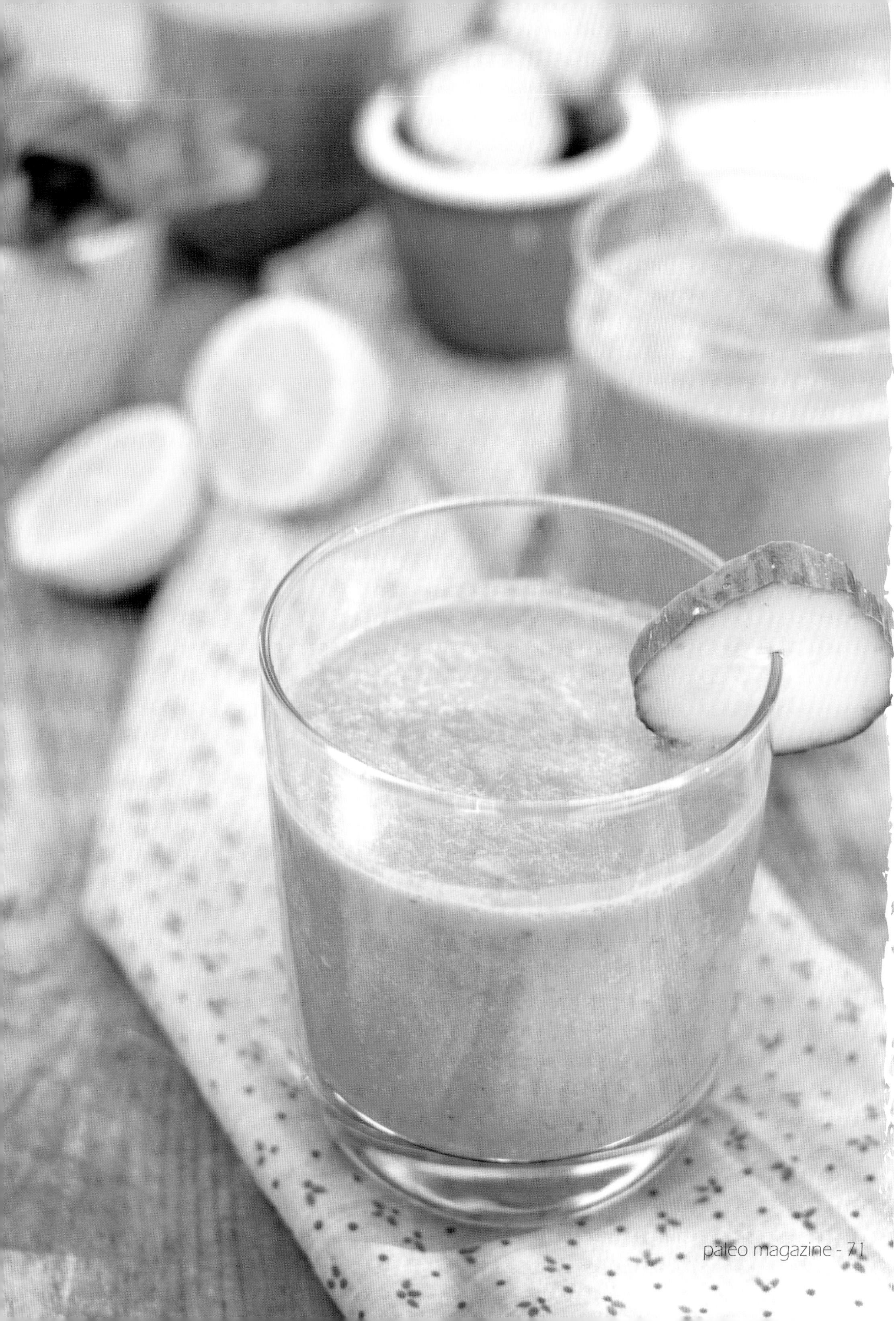

# Italian Meatballs

Estimated Prep Time: 15 minutes
Estimated Cooking Time:  minutes
Servings: 4

1 lb grass-fed ground beef
1 lb ground pork
1/2 medium onion, finely chopped
3 garlic cloves, minced
1/4 cup chopped fresh parsley
1/4 cup almond meal
2 Tbsp coconut flour
1 tsp oregano
1/2 tsp sea salt
1/2 tsp pepper
1/2 tsp basil
Pinch rosemary
2 Tbsp coconut oil
1/2 cup marinara sauce

1. Mix all ingredients in a bowl and roll into balls (about the size of golf balls).
2. In a large skillet, over medium-high heat, melt coconut oil. Add meatballs to skillet. Brown meatballs on all sides, about 8 minutes total.
3. Turn heat to low and add 1/2 cup marinara sauce. Watch for hot splatters! Stir gently and simmer for 5-10 minutes or until meatballs are cooked and sauce is heated through.

# Morning Egg Muffins

Estimated Prep Time: 15 minutes
Estimated Cooking Time: 30 minutes
Servings: 12

10 oz fresh baby spinach, cooked
1 large Roma tomato, diced
4 whole large eggs
4 egg whites
1 medium Vidalia onion
2 Tbsp finely chopped fresh parsley
2 Tbsp chia seeds
1/4 tsp sea salt
1/4 tsp freshly ground white pepper

1. Preheat oven to 350°F.
2. In a medium bowl, whisk eggs with egg whites. Add remaining ingredients and mix well to combine.
3. Prepare a muffin tin with nonstick baking spray. Pour egg mixture evenly into cups.
4. Bake for 30 minutes or until set. Set aside to cool.
5. Serve warm or store in the refrigerator.

As seen in:

# Nut-Free No'Oat Granola

Estimated Prep Time: 10 minutes
Estimated Cooking Time: 15 minutes
Servings: 4

1/2 cup organic raw pumpkin seeds
3/4 cup organic raw sunflower seed kernels
1/4 cup organic raisins
1/4 cup organic dried cherries
1/4 cup unsweetened organic coconut flakes
1 tsp pure vanilla extract
1/2 tsp pure almond extract
1/4 cup pure Grade B maple syrup

1. Mix all ingredients in a medium mixing bowl, coating everything well with the maple syrup.
2. Spread the mixture evenly on a parchment-lined baking sheet.
3. Bake in a 350°F oven for 12-15 minutes, or until coconut is golden. Stir once halfway.
4. Cool on a wire rack. If you feel a little crazy, toss in a few mini chocolate chips.
5. When completely cooled, mixture will be crunchy and delicious! Use as a snack or put some in a bowl with a little coconut milk for breakfast cereal.

As seen in:

PALEO
MAGAZINE
MODERN DAY PRIMAL LIFE

1-yr
Anniversary Issue!

Carbohydrate Conundrums
& Fat Fallacies
with Nora Gedgaudas

Digestive Issues
Overcome through diet

Pearly Whites
Diet and healthy teeth

Community Supported
Agriculture
Support your local farmer!

**The Food**
Nut Free Maple Granola
Recipes Moroccan
Almond Macaroons
Shrimp Ceviche
Egg Custard
Beef Brisket
Beet Kvass

# Paleo Chicken Wings

Estimated Prep Time: 15 minutes
Estimated Cooking Time: 45 minutes
Servings: 4

24 chicken wings, washed and patted dry
2 Tbsp coconut oil

**Seasoning:**
1 Tbsp paprika
2 tsp granulated onion
1/2 tsp granulated garlic
1/4 tsp smoked paprika
1 tsp sea salt
Freshly ground pepper to taste

**Wing Sauce:**
1 (15-oz) can organic tomato sauce
1 (6-oz) can organic tomato paste
3 Tbsp raw honey or maple syrup
3 Tbsp organic apple cider vinegar
2 tsp sea salt
1 Tbsp granulated onion
1 tsp paprika
1/2 tsp smoked paprika
2 tsp granulated garlic
1 Tbsp coconut aminos, gluten-free tamari soy sauce, or Bragg's liquid aminos

1. Mix wing seasoning ingredients in a small bowl.
2. Coat wings with coconut oil. Sprinkle the seasoning over wings and rub in evenly with your hands. Don't forget to wash your hands!
3. Cover a large baking sheet with foil and grease the foil. Place seasoned wings evenly on pan, trying to not let them touch so they bake evenly and get crispy.
4. Cook wings in a 375°F oven for about 45 minutes, or until wings are browned, crispy, and cooked through.
5. Meanwhile, combine all sauce ingredients in a large saucepan. Heat through on low-medium heat.
6. Place cooked wings in a large bowl, add sauce at your discretion, and toss lightly to coat wings. Serve and devour... and remember the napkins!
7. Refrigerate extra sauce to use with chicken fingers, steak bites, or mini meatloaf. You can even use it as a dipping sauce for Italian meatballs!

# Paleo Garden Burger

Estimated Prep Time: 25 minutes
Estimated Cooking Time: 10 minutes
Serves: 4

1 lb grass-fed ground beef
1/2 cup finely chopped yellow squash
1/2 cup finely chopped zucchini
1/3 cup finely chopped broccoli
1/4 cup finely chopped red onion
1/4 cup packed, finely chopped spinach
6 basil leaves, finely chopped
2 Tbsp finely chopped parsley
1 tsp granulated onion
1/2 tsp sea salt
Ground pepper
Coconut oil

1. Heat coconut oil in pan over medium heat.
2. Add onion and cook for 2-3 minutes.
3. Add broccoli and cook for 1-2 minutes.
4. Add carrot and cook for 2 minutes.
5. Add zucchini and yellow squash and cook for 2-3 minutes.
6. Add spinach and cook for 1 minute.
7. Remove pan from stove and allow veggie mixture to cool.
8. In large bowl, combine burger, veggies, basil, parsley, salt, pepper, and granulated onion and mix well.
9. Grill for about 5 minutes per side.
10. Top with avocado slices.

As seen online:

# Pork Tenderloin with Hearty Spice Rub

Estimated Prep Time: 10 minutes
Estimated Cooking Time: 30 minutes
Servings: 4

1 pork tenderloin
Chicken or beef broth
Maple syrup
Rosemary, fresh or dried
Turmeric
Pumpkin pie spice
Coconut oil
Sea salt
Freshly ground pepper

**THIS TENDERLOIN IS FAST AND EASY, AND IT'S EXCELLENT REHEATED.** We're not going to worry about measuring anything for it, either. Just trust yourself and add as much or as little as you think you need.

1. Preheat oven to 425°F.
2. Sprinkle loin with salt, pepper, rosemary, turmeric, and pumpkin pie spice. Rub in well.
3. In a large ovenproof skillet, melt coconut oil over medium-high heat and sear loin on all sides.
4. Turn off heat. Add broth to pan, scraping any bits from the pan as you do. Pour a little maple syrup on the loin.
5. Cover and place in 425°F oven for 20-30 minutes, or until done, depending on thickness of loin.
6. Let rest for 10 minutes, slice, and serve.

As seen in:

**PALEO**
MAGAZINE
MODERN DAY PRIMAL LIFE

**Intermittent Fasting**
The importance of not eating

**Paleo New Year**
Start your year off right

**"Safe Starches"**
Rice is nice?

**The Food**
Curry Crab Dip
Cantonese Wraps
Pork Tenderloin
Coconut Bark

NORCAL
STRENGTH &
CONDITIONING

Feb/Mar 2012

**Robb Wolf**
Q&A with the
Paleo movement's Big Daddy

# Quick Breakfast Sausage

Estimated Prep Time: 5 minutes
Estimated Cooking Time: 10 minutes
Servings: 8

1 lb grass-fed ground beef
2 Tbsp raw honey
2 tsp dried parsley
1 tsp marjoram
1 tsp granulated onion
1 tsp paprika
1 tsp fennel seeds
1/2 tsp sage
1/2 tsp sea salt
1/4 tsp turmeric
Pepper, freshly ground, to taste
1 tsp coconut oil

1. Heat oil in pan over medium heat.
2. In a small bowl, mix all ingredients and form into approximately 3" patties.
3. Cook over medium heat for 2-3 minutes.
4. Flip and cook for another 3 minutes.

## Variation: Italian Sausage

Add the following to the above ingredients:
1 Tbsp Italian spices
2 tsp granulated garlic
1 tsp granulated onion
1/8 tsp cayenne pepper

As seen in:

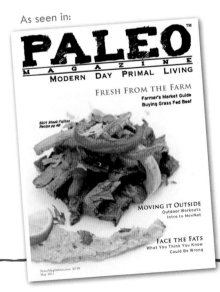

# Sea Salt and Chive Crackers

Estimated Prep Time: 20 minutes
Estimated Cooking Time: 15 minutes
Serves: Makes 56 crackers

**Dry ingredients:**
1/3 cup coconut flour
1/2 flax meal (ground, organic, golden flax seeds)
Pinch sea salt (plus more for tops)
Pepper, freshly ground, to taste

**Wet ingredients:**
1 clove garlic, pressed
2 eggs
1 Tbsp melted coconut oil

**Add-ins:**
3 Tbsp chopped fresh chives

1. Preheat oven to 350°F.
2. In a medium bowl, whisk together dry ingredients.
3. Add the egg and pressed garlic, and mix well with a hand mixer.
4. With the mixer on low, add coconut oil slowly and blend well. Let dough sit for 5 minutes to thicken if necessary.
5. Press dough with your hands to form a ball. Place onto a piece of parchment paper, large enough to line a baking sheet. Use a second sheet of parchment paper on top of the dough and roll into a rectangle to 1/4" thickness. Try to make it as even as possible so the edges aren't too thin, as they can burn easily. Remove top sheet.
6. Using a sharp knife, score the dough lengthwise into 7 rows then across into 8 rows.
7. Bake 7 minutes, then pull the tray out and separate the crackers carefully with a spatula. Return tray to the oven and bake 8-10 minutes, or until centers are cooked and edges are golden.
8. Cool on the tray on a wire rack. Store in an airtight container for up to 5 days or freeze up to a month.

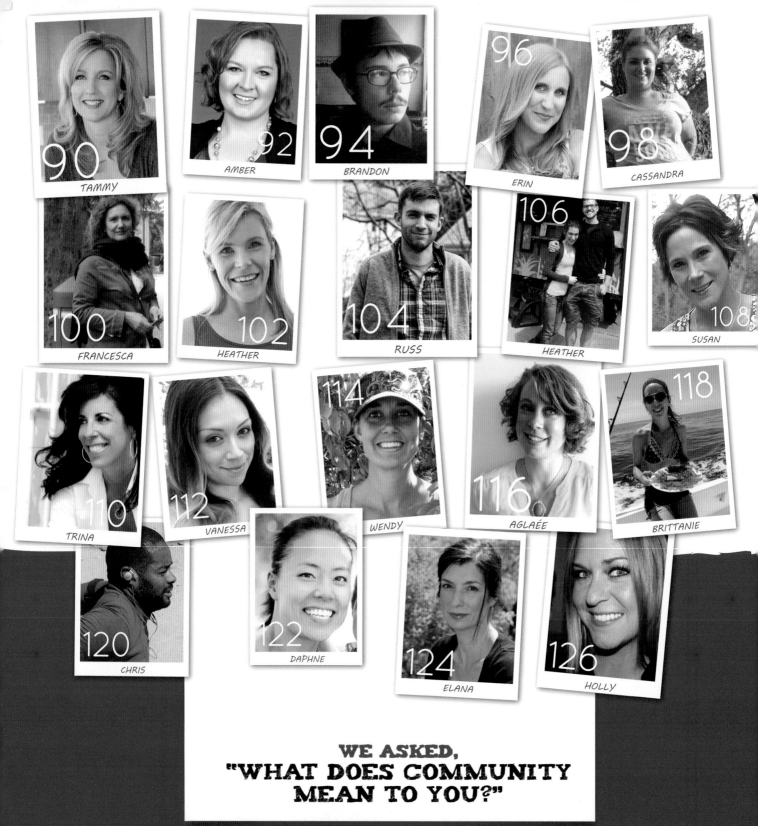

90 TAMMY

92 AMBER

94 BRANDON

96 ERIN

98 CASSANDRA

100 FRANCESCA

102 HEATHER

104 RUSS

106 HEATHER

108 SUSAN

110 TRINA

112 VANESSA

114 WENDY

116 AGLAÉE

118 BRITTANIE

120 CHRIS

122 DAPHNE

124 ELANA

126 HOLLY

## WE ASKED, "WHAT DOES COMMUNITY MEAN TO YOU?"

"Those who encourage me to be the best version of me - the way I was born to be. Supportive, understanding, non judgmental."
@JenKlouse (Twitter)

"Sharing, empathy, compassion, support, accountability, trust, growth, and care."
@JeromiePreas (Twitter)

128 KAREN

130 NAZANIN

132 MARGARET

134 KELLY

136 LAURA

138 MARY

140 KATRINA

142 KYLE

144 KIMBERLY

146 SHANTI

148 MICHELLE

150 MICHELLE

152 KELLY

154 NELL

156 KELLY

158 KEIRSTEN

160 KRISTEN

162 REBEKAH

164 SARAH

166 MAUREEN

"PEOPLE WHO SUPPORT UR EFFORTS & CHEER YOU ON EVEN IF THEY DON'T BELIEVE IN THE SAME CAUSE - THEIR FOCUS IS ON BUILDING U."
@SUMMERSDAZE (TWITTER)

"Support and encouragement!"
Pam J. (Facebook)

"Trust and vulnerability."
@hmulholland (Twitter)

Family Encouragement Acceptance Love Support Survival Trust Truth Motivation Accountability Healing Growth Success.
@DavidHamilton77 (Twitter)

# Tammy Credicott
### BEND, OR

About six years ago, the dynamic of my family life changed over the span of only a few months, and things got very complicated, very quickly.

My husband and kids were diagnosed with everything from celiac disease, ADD, and dermatitis to various food intolerances and night terrors. For most of the following year, we spent every minute trying to figure it all out and answer the dozens of questions in our minds. Why are the kids tired all the time? Are we sure it's ADD? Do we try prescriptions or natural methods? And the big question: What the heck are we going to eat now? I'm still not sure how we survived that very stressful period. But we did survive and – I can honestly say now – thrived, after the initial shock wore off.

Needless to say, my cooking and baking methods have changed over the years, and the delicious successes have been a result of trial and error, family memories, and lots of cravings! But I'm not a chef. I'm a self-taught home cook who loves good food, and even more, loves food that is good for us. And while I've never received formal training, what I have done is conquer my fear of cooking and baking without gluten, grains, or dairy. I have figured out shortcuts that make my family life much easier. I have found ways to send my kids to school and birthday parties knowing they have a yummy treat that won't make them sick.

Changing the way we eat healed my family. My husband is no longer suffering and sick from gluten. My youngest very quickly started sleeping through the night again, and her dermatitis vanished. My oldest started to regain verbal skills I thought were gone forever, and her ability to focus, both at school and at home, improved dramatically. My family is healthier and happier, because food is no longer our enemy. For us, taking control of our health meant taking control of our diet. And I'm oh-so-happy we did!

www.TheHealthyGFLife.com

# Berry Shortcakes & Whipped Cream

Estimated Prep Time: 20 minutes
Estimated Cooking Time: 15 minutes
Servings: 8-10

**Shortcakes:**

2 cup raw walnuts
1 cup raw pumpkin seeds
1/4 cup coconut flour
2 Tbsp arrowroot starch
1/4 cup freshly ground flax meal
1 tsp cinnamon
2 tsp baking soda
1/2 tsp sea salt
4 eggs
3 Tbsp honey
1-1/2 tsp pure vanilla extract
1/4 tsp pure almond extract
1/3 cup coconut oil
1/3 cup coconut milk

**Whipped Cream:**

1 can coconut milk
1 tsp pure vanilla extract
1 Tbsp coconut nectar or honey
1 Tbsp coconut flour

**Shortcakes:**

1. In a food processor, puree walnuts and pumpkin seeds into a fine meal.
2. In a medium bowl, whisk together walnut/seed meal, coconut flour, arrowroot, flax meal, cinnamon, baking soda, and sea salt. Set aside.
3. In a mixer with a paddle attachment, beat eggs until frothy. Add honey, vanilla and almond extracts, coconut oil and coconut milk. Mix until just blended.
4. Add dry ingredients to mixer, a little at a time, until fully incorporated. Mix on high for about 30 seconds or until well blended.
5. Scoop dough with an ice cream scoop and place on a parchment lined baking sheet.
6. Bake in a 350°F oven for about 15 minutes, or until browned and firm in the center when touched. Cool completely.

**To assemble cakes:**

1. Slice cakes in half lengthwise. Place bottom half on a plate and spoon sliced strawberries (or your favorite summer berries) over cake.
2. Place top half of cake on top of strawberries.
3. Spoon more strawberries on top. Drizzle coconut whipped cream over shortcakes. Devour!

**Whipped Cream:**

1. For best results, refrigerate coconut milk and freeze a stainless steel bowl and beaters for a hand mixer for about 30 minutes before blending.
2. Put all ingredients into the cold stainless steel bowl. Blend on high for about 3 minutes, until thickened.

# Amber Beam
### ARLINGTON, VA

Not so long ago, I was a trapped in a vicious cycle of takeout meals and antacids. I followed the Standard American Diet, complete with low-fat yogurt, whole-grain sandwiches, and pasta dinners. I had become discouraged by my inability to lose weight, despite consistent workouts and calorie cutting, until my trainer turned me on to Paleo and a world filled with pork chops, omelets, and bacon. Needless to say, I haven't turned back!

As an avid foodie and lover of all things epicurean, I had watched numerous cooking shows but rarely ventured into the kitchen to make a meal. Paleo changed me from a kitchen bystander to a floundering cook. Refusing to give in to sub standard convenience foods, I taught myself to cook easy Paleo meals that tasted great. The meals had to be easy and satisfying for me and my (not-yet-Paleo) husband. After several months of intense recipe development and testing, I wrote and self published "Weeknight Paleo: 9 Weeks of Quick and Easy Gluten-Free Meals", a cookbook that helps busy cooks (and novices) get quick, easy, and tasty Paleo meals on the table in 30 minutes or less.

My blog, Paleo Savvy (www.PaleoSavvy.com), highlights my culinary trials and tribulations, while giving readers the confidence and know-how to get in the kitchen and make a fantastic meal. The blog tackles tips and tricks for everything from slaying spaghetti squash to cooking the best bacon EVER! With a few culinary tricks and a solid recipe, I prove that even on your busiest weeknight, you can make a stress-free, delicious Paleo dinner the entire family will enjoy!

# Asian Chicken Soup with Napa Cabbage & Bok Choy

Estimated Prep Time: 10 minutes
Estimated Cooking Time: 15 minutes
Servings: 4

1 Tbsp sesame oil
3 cloves garlic, minced
1-1/2 Tbsp ginger, peeled and minced
1 lb boneless, skinless chicken,
  diced into 1-inch cubes
5 cups chicken stock
1-1/2 Tbsp fish sauce
2 Tbsp gluten-free soy sauce
1 carrot, cut into ribbons using vegetable peeler
1/2 head napa cabbage, chopped
2 stalks bok choy, thinly sliced
1 Tbsp lime juice
Salt, pepper to taste

**MEANT TO WARM YOU FROM THE INSIDE OUT,** this Asian spin on traditional chicken noodle soup is sure to break the winter deep freeze or soothe that scratchy throat you feel coming on. Ginger and garlic make the broth sing and the vegetables add body and vitamins.

1. In a large saucepan, heat the oil over medium-high heat.
2. Add the garlic and ginger, and sauté until fragrant, for about 30 seconds.
3. Add the chicken and cook until golden brown on all sides, for 5 to 7 minutes.
4. Add the stock, fish sauce, and soy sauce, and bring to a boil.
5. Add the carrots, napa cabbage, and bok choy. Cook until the bok choy is tender, for 2 to 3 minutes.
6. Remove from heat and stir in the lime juice. Season with salt and pepper and serve.

# Brandon Chapple

NASHVILLE, TN

I owe my entire Paleo lifestyle to being hired at www.MissDots.com, a healthy-eating startup in Nashville, TN. While working from home, I'm able to really focus on my healthy eating goals. I grew up in a standard American household, with a lot of fast food and processed food. It was a pretty gloomy time. My recent change to Paleo, however, has been very positive. Getting healthy has been a goal of mine for over a decade, and going Paleo finally makes me feel like I'm on the right path.

I'm really spontaneous with the foods I buy and cook, and since I started working from home, I've had the time to keep things healthy and have some fun in the kitchen. I go to the grocery store roughly as often as I did before going Paleo, but I buy a lot more when I'm there. I'll usually grab random proteins and veggies and find a way to make it all tasty.

It's hard to judge how my life has changed since going Paleo since it happened in tandem with a complete change in occupation and lifestyle. I went from taking two buses across town to get to work and back (shoveling fast food along the way) to working from home, completely on my own schedule. Just that change alone has made me much happier. I'm so blessed to have been given the opportunity to learn how to master Paleo cooking.

# Paleo-Friendly Mayo

Estimated Prep Time: 5 minutes
Estimated Cooking Time: N/A
Servings: 1 cup

1 large egg yolk
1/4 tsp salt
1/4 tsp Dijon mustard
1-1/2 tsp lemon juice
1 tsp white vinegar
3/4 cup walnut oil

**THE HEALTHY-EATING STARTUP I WORK FOR** is heavily influenced by French cooking, but their recipes call for a lot of Vegenaise, which is definitely not Paleo-friendly due to the grapeseed oil. I came up with this quick, easy homemade mayo as an alternative, and it's taken my remoulade sauces, chicken salads, and burgers to the next level!

1. In a medium bowl, combine all the ingredients except for the oil.
2. Using a whisk or electric hand mixer, beat the egg-yolk mixture vigorously for about 30 seconds, until the color brightens.
3. Mixing continuously, add the oil very slowly, a third of a cup at a time, adding the last third of a cup all at once.
4. Continue beating until the mayo starts to thicken, then cool in the refrigerator until it's thickened even more.

# Erin Walker

LEAGUE CITY, TX

Growing up, my meals consisted of pizza, tacos, pasta, and Chinese takeout. My unhealthy lifestyle caught up with me when I got to college, and I ended up in the emergency room with unexplained chest pain. It turned out that I had gallstones and my next step was gallbladder surgery. After my surgery, I continued eating the same way, but I wasn't digesting my food well at all. I had constant stomachaches and took Imodium ALL the time. After seven years of pain, I decided enough was enough.

I wanted to force myself into liking vegetables and eating a healthier diet, so I tried a cleanse. Well, the cleanse worked! Kind of… After I finished, I felt great and was eating better than ever before. But I started introducing "cheat meals" into my diet a few weeks after the cleanse. Any time I ate grains, or dairy, I would have severe stomach pain and bloating. I told myself this was normal and that my body would have to get used to eating that kind of food again. After six months of extreme pain, Tums, and Beano, I wasn't getting any better, so I went to a nutritional consultant/herbalist who put me on a strict Paleo diet.

In short, eating Paleo has changed my life. My stomach inflammation has subsided enough that I can finally eat without any pain!

When I embraced the Paleo lifestyle, though, I truly missed eating desserts. I would walk by my favorite cupcake bakery and feel sad that I'd never be able to eat there again. I wished so many times for a bakery that could accommodate my dietary restrictions, but I couldn't find a single one, so my husband and I opened Little E's Kitchen to help fill that void for people with similar dietary restrictions. At Little E's, I bake Paleo cupcakes and sell them locally. I also teach first grade and my coworkers ask a lot of questions about the Paleo diet, which inspired me to start a blog to share the recipes I create with my friends and family. Since starting the blog, I've had quite a few people ask me to bake them gf/df/Paleo desserts for birthdays, anniversaries, or just for fun.

# Cinnamon Crumble Coffee Cake

Estimated Prep Time: 20 minutes
Estimated Cooking Time: 45 minutes
Servings: 6 to 8

1 cup almond flour
1/4 cup plus 1 Tbsp coconut flour
2 eggs
1 heaping tsp vanilla
1/4 cup honey
1/2 cup water
1/2 cup plus 2 Tbsp coconut milk
1/4 tsp baking soda
1/4 tsp salt

**Crumble Topping:**
3 Tbsp ghee or butter
1/3 cup coconut palm sugar
4-1/2 Tbsp almond flour
1/4 tsp salt
2 tsp cinnamon
1 Tbsp honey

## GROWING UP, MY FAVORITE BREAKFAST WAS always cinnamon coffee cake.

This recipe is dairy free and gluten free, and uses all-natural sweeteners. This and the other recipes I post on my blog are ones that keep my inflammation in check and don't hurt my stomach. Even if you don't have any dietary restrictions, this recipe is just plain ol' good!
www.LittleEKitchen.blogspot.com

1. Preheat oven to 350°F.
2. Mix all the wet ingredients (eggs, vanilla, honey, water, milk) in a small bowl.
3. Mix the dry ingredients (almond flour, coconut flour, salt, baking soda) in another bowl.
4. Combine the wet ingredients and dry ingredients. Stir until free of lumps.
5. Grease a loaf pan.
6. Add half of the batter to the loaf pan.
7. Melt ghee/butter. Add the palm sugar, almond flour, salt, cinnamon, and honey to the ghee. Stir the crumble mixture. It should be crumbly. If not, add more almond flour, one tablespoon at a time.
8. Evenly sprinkle 3/4 of the crumble mixture over the batter in the loaf pan.
9. Pour the rest of the batter over the crumble mixture until it's fully covered.
10. Sprinkle the rest of the crumble mixture over the top of the coffee cake.
11. Bake for 45 minutes or until the edges are brown and a toothpick comes out clean.

# Cassandra Plank

LUBBOCK, TX

In June of 2011 I made the realization that I was too young to be feeling so tired all the time, and I needed a way to lose the weight that had crept up on me from my whole-grain-rich vegetarian diet. I chose to go Paleo because it was the opposite of everything that wasn't working for me at the time, and I jumped in headfirst with no transitional period.

Adding fat was difficult initially because I had been indoctrinated to avoid it like the plague. But once I realized how satiating fat could be, I stopped thinking about food constantly. I began to feel in tune with my level of satiety in a way I hadn't before, which improved my relationship with food. I dropped weight rapidly the first few months and began to feel more energized throughout the day.

One challenge was going out to eat and handling social pressures to indulge. I got in the habit of looking at restaurant menus before going out so I had a plan of action. My closest friends and family have come to accept the way I eat and don't tempt me with the bread basket at restaurants anymore!

I've dropped a few dress sizes, but this change has also had many non-scale benefits. My favorite change has been my skin, which has cleared up a lot. My blood sugar doesn't crash like it used to after pasta or bread, so I feel more emotionally balanced. Feeling healthy and energetic has also had a positive effect on my mood and the way I interact with others socially and professionally.

I spend more time on food preparation, but it's worth it because the payoff is more energy to complete everything I want in the day, from school work to graduate research and being able to top all that off with a workout. My experience with weight loss and Paleo have shown me there is no "one size fits all" when it comes to eating. By going against conventional wisdom's low-fat, grain-based recommendations, I found something that's healthy and functional for a busy graduate student like myself.

# Autumn Turkey Salad with Golden Raisin Vinaigrette

Estimated Prep Time: 15 minutes
Estimated Cooking Time: N/A
Servings: 4

**For the dressing:**
3 Tbsp apple cider vinegar
3-1/2 Tbsp golden raisins
6 Tbsp extra-virgin olive oil
1/8 tsp celery seeds
Salt and pepper, to taste

**For the salad:**
1 pear, any color, diced
1 cup chopped celery
1 cup halved grapes, any variety
8 cups loosely packed mixed baby lettuce
12 oz cooked turkey breast, sliced
1/4 cup chopped walnuts

**AUTUMN IS MY FAVORITE TIME OF YEAR,** not only for the changing leaves but also for the incoming produce. This salad pays homage to my favorite fall fruit, grapes, by featuring both fresh grapes and raisins. The sweet and tangy flavor of the dressing is a nice counterpoint to savory turkey (such as leftovers from your Thanksgiving feast). Plus, the ingredients provide an array of delightful textures, from the crunch of the walnuts and celery to the buttery softness of the lettuce and pears.

1. To prepare the dressing, combine all the ingredients except the celery seeds in a blender or mini food processor and blend.
2. When the raisins are finely chopped and the dressing is emulsified, stir in the celery seeds, taste for seasoning, then set aside.
3. In a large bowl, add the pear, celery, grapes, and lettuce. Toss with just enough dressing to coat.
4. Divide the salad among four serving plates. Top each with slices of turkey, drizzle on a little more dressing, and sprinkle the walnuts on top. Serve immediately.

# Francesca Caricato

### SANTA MARINELLA, ITALY

I've always struggled with weight loss: I was an overweight child ("Eat it—you need to grow up!"), an overweight teenager who hid her body under baggy clothes, and an overworked, overstressed overweight woman. When I became a mother, I was intrigued by nutrition, and even studied nutritional science. I began to eat better, discovered yoga and swimming, and left my job to be a housewife and stay-at-home mother. That was the first big health change in my life.

Approaching menopause, however, I started developing anemia and PCOS. In the meantime, my diet (and therefore my family's) began to deviate toward vegetarianism, and after a year of cereals and legumes my anemia had worsened. At this point I discovered the Paleo diet, thanks to Robb Wolf's book. As well as resolving my anemia and hormonal imbalances, it gave me a chance to learn how to handle my weight.

I'm still a bit overweight (I probably eat a little too much fruit and seeds) but I'm undoubtedly fitter and healthier now at nearly 50 than I was at 25! You won't find pasta or bread in my kitchen—which is unbelievable for an Italian family!—even if my husband and my son won't give up their Saturday take-away pizza. That's okay with me, but they're always obligated to pick me up a roast chicken!

# Fennelled
# Paleo Chicken

Estimated Prep Time: 30 minutes
Estimated Cooking Time: 25 minutes
Servings: 2

1 chicken breast
1 fennel bulb
1/4 cup coconut milk
1 drop anise liqueur (sambuca, ouzo, absinthe,
   arak, raki, pastis, etc.)
Olive or coconut oil
Salt

1. Set aside the fennel beards (green sprouts)
   and slice the rest of the fennel; let it boil in
   salted water.
2. Slice the chicken breasts into nuggets, let
   them brown in a pan with oil and salt, then
   set them aside to deglaze the pan with a
   drop of sambuca (or other anise liqueur).
3. Add the coconut milk, fennel beards, and the
   nuggets. Let it thicken and serve with slices
   of boiled fennel.

I was bored of fennel salad and roasted chicken breast, so I decided to **ENHANCE THE ANISE SCENT OF RAW FENNEL WITH A LIQUEUR** very popular in my city. It's only a drop—just the perfume—but it does the trick!

# Heather Connell

CHARLOTTE, NC

I'm Heather: a wife, a mom, a food blogger, and a lover of Paleo cooking. However, a few years ago, this was not how I cooked.

A little over a year after the birth of my twin daughters, I started experiencing stomach pains, fatigue, and several other health problems that left me feeling horrible. After five or six months of monthly doctor's visits to monitor all these suspicious symptoms, I became increasingly frustrated and tired. The doctor finally said my choice was to either go on medication or be faced with surgery.

Frustrated and scared, I decided to research the "whys" of what I was feeling. I soon found out that many of the issues were coming from my very own kitchen and all the foods I loved and thought were right for me. I began to remove culprits from my diet and gradually started to feel better, but it wasn't until I stumbled across Paleo that I started to feel fantastic. All the health problems that had once ailed me disappeared in about a month, and it was almost like I could see more clearly—a beautiful thing when you've felt so foggy for so long. I felt like a new person who'd been given a second chance!

As much as I loved this new feeling, my kitchen had become foreign to me, and the things I used to love to eat were now forbidden. In a way, I had to learn to cook all over again, so I got back in the kitchen and embraced my new lifestyle. One beautiful aspect of this new journey was having my twin daughters by my side. We found ourselves creating delicious meals using only seasonal whole foods and local grass-fed and pastured proteins. Not only was I teaching myself, but I was helping my daughters learn the importance of real, whole foods and taking care of our health.

I've shared every step of my two-year-plus journey with the readers of my blog, www.MultiplyDelicious.com, from my recipes to the reasons behind my new lifestyle. I'm a firm believer that as Paleo eaters, we can still eat foods that make our hearts smile and our stomachs dance with delight.

# Moroccan Meatballs with Citrus-Glazed Carrots

Estimated Prep Time: 10 minutes
Estimated Cooking Time: 25 minutes
Servings: 6 to 8

I love incorporating various spices into my cooking, and this recipe was developed by experimenting with a number of different spices. **JUST ONE BITE WILL CREATE A BURST OF EXOTIC FLAVORS IN YOUR MOUTH!**

2 tsp olive oil
3 to 4 large carrots, peeled and cut into
  1/2-inch wide and 2-inch long matchsticks
1 orange, juiced and zested
1 lb 85% grass-fed ground beef
1 egg white
3 cloves garlic, minced
1/8 cup blanched almond flour
1 Tbsp ground coriander
1/2 Tbsp fresh mint, minced
1 tsp ground cumin
3/4 tsp ground cinnamon
1/2 tsp sea salt
Fresh ground black pepper

1. In a medium nonstick skillet, heat oil on medium heat for 1 minute. Add carrots and sauté, stirring occasionally, for about 5 minutes.
2. Stir in orange juice and 1 teaspoon orange zest. Cover, reduce heat to low, and simmer for 8 minutes, until carrots are slightly softened. Remove from heat and keep covered.
3. In a large bowl, combine beef, egg white, garlic, almond meal, coriander, fresh mint, cumin, cinnamon, salt, and pepper. With hands or a fork, mix well to combine and shape into 12 to 15 meatballs.
4. Heat a large nonstick skillet on medium heat. Working in batches, add meatballs and cook for 7 to 8 minutes, making sure to brown evenly; don't overcrowd the skillet. Meatballs are fully cooked when completely opaque in center. Place cooked meatballs on a plate with a paper towel until all the meatballs are cooked.
5. Serve meatballs over, or alongside, the carrots.

# Russ Crandall

GLEN BURNIE, MD

My family started a Paleo lifestyle in 2010, after I had suffered through several years of medical issues, including a stroke and being diagnosed with a rare autoimmune disorder called Takayasu's Arteritis. The positive effect of the diet on my health was profound and immediate, and today I am no longer taking most of the medications that I had thought I needed just to remain stable. My doctors still can't figure out how I just suddenly started getting better one day.

We adopted the diet as a family as a way to keep bad (tempting!) ingredients out of the house, but unexpectedly my wife and son benefited from the change in diet as well. My wife lost weight and found a better balance in energy levels, and my then-toddler son immediately started displaying a more even, calm behavior — which he still has today.

After following the diet for a number of years, focusing on nutrient-rich foods like bone broth, offal, and fermented veggies has improved our health dramatically. When first switching to Paleo, even a bit of gluten would immediately make us feel terrible. However, over time we've built up a fair amount of resiliency, likely thanks to improved gut flora, and we aren't as effected by disruptions in our diet anymore. This has been a major boon to us since we are now able to feel great while still dipping into the "gray" areas of Paleo (ice cream!) from time to time.

www.TheDomesticMan.com

# Gas-Grilled Beef Back Ribs

Estimated Prep Time: 40 minutes

Estimated Cooking Time: 3 hours

Servings: 6

2 racks beef back ribs (approx. 8 lbs)
1 Tbsp black pepper
1/2 Tbsp salt
1 tsp each ground mustard, paprika, cumin
1/2 tsp each curry powder, onion powder,
   garlic powder, cayenne pepper, and cinnamon
1 large handful mesquite wood chips

**BEEF BACK RIBS DON'T GET AS MUCH ATTENTION AS PORK RIBS,** and for good reason: Getting tender, delicious beef ribs is often harder than making pork ribs because they require a low-and-slow method of cooking that is intimidating to many cooks. This recipe provides high-quality ribs using basic grilling methods that are already available to most home chefs!

1. Combine all the dry ingredients. Sprinkle the dry rub over both sides of the ribs and let them sit at room temperature for 30 minutes. As the ribs are setting, take a large handful of mesquite wood chips and soak them in water for 30 minutes.

2. To get a good amount of smoke going, add the soaked chips to a smoker box and place the box under the grill grates on one side of the grill (directly under a burner). Preheat your grill for about 10 minutes, then leave only the burner under the smoke box running.

3. Place the ribs on the opposite end of the smoker box (the cool side of the grill) and cover. Adjust the burner's intensity to get a grill temperature of as close to 265°F as possible. Grill the ribs using this indirect method for 3 hours.

4. After 3 hours, the ribs should look slightly crispy on the outside and most of the fat should have cooked off the meat. Turn all of the burners up to medium heat and grill the ribs on direct heat for a couple minutes, to crisp up the remaining fat. This should only take a few moments once the heat is going. Brush on some barbecue sauce and remove the ribs from the grill.

5. Slice the ribs into singles using kitchen shears and enjoy!

# Heather Hunter

PORTLAND, OR

Two years ago, I was working in a bagel shop in Portland, Oregon. I took four to six sugars in my coffee and had regular doughnut-eating competitions with my coworkers. I usually won. It was in this coffee shop that I met my partner, Joe, who totally changed my life. He had been following the Paleo diet and had a clear grasp on nutrition science and the food-body connection that I hadn't seen before.

It wasn't long before I was on the Paleo wagon myself. For the first time ever, this skinny girl felt strong and healthy, and my mood (read: blood sugar) stabilized. Eight months later I dropped out of business school, we both quit our jobs, and we opened Cultured Caveman (www.CulturedCavemanPDX.com), the West Coast's first 100-percent Paleo-friendly food cart! Opening a food cart forced us to quickly figure out how to make large batches of food without a lot of prep time in a space half the size of our home kitchen. We even render our own grass-fed beef tallow right in the cart!

A little more than a year later, we've opened two more carts in other parts of town and now have a staff of seven! The Paleo lifestyle has completely changed my life for the better, both personally and professionally. I've found a loving and supportive community of people who care about their health and we really have the best customers anyone could ask for. No more bagels for this Cavema'am.

# Kale Salad

Estimated Prep Time: 45 minutes
Estimated Cooking Time: 1 hour (in fridge)
Servings: 12

2/3 lb kale
2/3 lb carrots
1/3 lb purple cabbage
1/4 cup apple cider vinegar
2/3 cup olive oil
2/3 cup lemon juice
45 g fresh ginger
1 tsp sea salt

1. Peel and finely mince ginger.
2. Mix ginger with olive oil, apple cider vinegar, lemon juice, and salt.
3. Using either a food processor or hand grater, shred the purple cabbage and carrots. Add to dressing.
4. Wash and devein kale.
5. Cut kale into small bite-sized strips and add to dressing.
6. Mix everything well.
7. Refrigerate for at least 1 hour.
8. Enjoy!

A light and bright, fresh and tangy salad.
**ALL-RAW INGREDIENTS MAKE THIS SALAD EXTRA CRISP AND NUTRITIOUS!**

# Susan Napolitano

MONROE, CT

I've always been passionate about food, and over the years this passion has manifested in different ways. As a kid it meant I ate everything in sight, a feat I was able to accomplish and still maintain my skinny self. In my twenties I began to spread my wings in the kitchen, and prided myself on making everything low fat and "healthy." I incorporated whole-wheat pasta, soy products, Greek yogurt, and just about anything labeled "fat-free" into my diet and cooking.

Once I had kids I started to think a little more about food quality. I leaned away from processed stuff and toward more sustainable and organic products. All the while I gave off the impression of being healthy. I was physically fit, and looked well. I felt like I was doing everything right, but I didn't feel as good as I thought I should.

I'd always struggled with autoimmune issues, but I hit rock bottom after the birth of my second child in 2006. I started thyroid treatment, and every day was a constant battle to feel balanced. Out went the gluten. Then the dairy. Then my marriage. It was the hardest time in my life. I ran my adrenals into the ground, and wound up with an ankle fracture from literally trying to run my stress away.

Seeking a fresh start, I enrolled in nutrition school and immersed myself in the food-body connection. I dabbled in different diets, from veganism to macrobiotics. Finally my search lead me to Paleo.

The light bulb went off, and the changes began. My stomach pains ceased. My energy skyrocketed. During the two years I've lived Paleo, I've reduced my thyroid dose twice, and have watched my cholesterol levels continually improve. I'm eating more fat than ever before in my life, yet I'm at my leanest.

My kids are so used to my cooking crazy concoctions that they didn't really notice the transition. My good eaters don't notice a difference between a grain-free and a "regular" pancake. We always have an open dialogue about whole foods and nutrition.

I began my blog www.PreppyPaleo.com as a personal endeavor, as I wanted a virtual catalogue of my kitchen experiments. I honestly never expected to gain a following! I hope to keep sharing and growing, and would love to publish my own cookbook.

# Paleo Breakfast Cookies

Estimated Prep Time: 10 minutes
Estimated Cooking Time: 15 minutes
Servings: 12 to 15

1 cup raw almond butter or
  organic sunflower seed butter
1 egg
1/4 cup raw honey or maple syrup
3 cups total mix-ins of choice (such as unsweetened
  shredded coconut, raw cacao nibs, sunflower
  seeds, raisins, or hulled hemp hearts)
1/2 tsp vanilla
1/2 tsp cinnamon
1/2 tsp baking soda
1/4 tsp salt

**THIS RECIPE WAS BORN OUT OF A DESIRE TO COME UP WITH A KID-FRIENDLY BREAKFAST TREAT** I could always have on hand for me and my family—and these cookies freeze beautifully. They've been a huge hit on my website, and have since spawned a pumpkin version. One reader also shared that she crumbles her "batter" to create a Paleo granola.

1. Preheat oven to 350°F.
2. Combine all ingredients in a stand mixer until thoroughly blended.
3. Drop by tablespoons onto a greased or Silpat-lined baking sheet. Press down lightly with hand.
4. Bake for 12 to 15 minutes.
5. Allow to cool on wire rack. Enjoy!

# Trina Beck

PHOENIX, AZ

Since transitioning to the Paleo lifestyle in January 2013, my husband and I have enjoyed the many rewards that come with sticking to wholesome foods while steering clear of all wheat, dairy, legumes, refined sugars, vegetable oils, and processed foods.

While we've never considered ourselves "bad" eaters, and fortunately have never been more than a few pounds overweight from time to time, switching to the Paleo lifestyle has brought us many positive—and a few unexpected—rewards.

The first change I noticed was more energy to get through my 10-hour workdays. I'm constantly on the go at the office, and I believe the nutrient-dense foods and fewer empty carbs I'm now eating give me the fuel I need to push through even the busiest days. I've had digestive issues my whole life—nothing serious, but enough to be annoying and slow me down. Since going Paleo, though, my digestive tract is much happier. And at night, I tend to fall asleep faster and sleep more soundly, and then wake up refreshed and ready to tackle a new day. One of the biggest surprises of getting on a Paleo regimen is my seasonal allergies have practically vanished. That's amazing considering daily sneezing fits and watery eyes were the norm when the pollen count was sky-high here in Arizona.

When we first switched to the Paleo lifestyle, one of our biggest panics was not knowing what to prepare for lunch. Breakfast was easy with eggs, and dinner was no problem with meat and veggies, but figuring out something Paleo other than a salad when you're so used to grabbing a sandwich at lunch was perplexing. I've been an avid cook my whole life, and here I was struggling to come up with something as simple as lunch! That's one of the reasons I started my first blog, www.PaleoNewbie.com, to share Paleo recipes anyone can whip up that are delicious, nutritious and hopefully a little different than the standard Paleo fare.

I hope you enjoy this easy recipe. The combination of flavors is really awesome and so good for you, too! Finally, I'd like to wish everyone good health and continued success on your lifelong Paleo journey!

110 - recipes

# Spicy Grilled Stuffed Avocado

Estimated Prep Time: 20 minutes
Estimated Cooking Time: 7 minutes
Servings: 4

1-1/2 tsp paprika
1 tsp cayenne
1 tsp salt
1/2 tsp onion powder
1/2 tsp garlic powder
1/2 tsp thyme
1/2 tsp basil
1/2 tsp pepper
1 Tbsp hot sauce, any kind
2 Tbsp olive oil
Juice of 2 limes
3 Tbsp chopped cilantro (leaves only)
2 avocados
20-plus medium raw peeled shrimp.
  I always cook more because everyone loves them!
1 tomato, seeded and chopped small
1/4 cup diced red onion
1 small red chili pepper, diced small (I prefer jalapeño)
Salt and pepper
Wood skewers soaked in water, or metal skewers

## I'VE ALWAYS LOVED THE CREAMY TASTE AND HEALTHY FAT IN AVOCADOS. This recipe is a great way to add a tasty side dish or appetizer to your meal if you're already planning on firing up the grill for steaks or seafood.

1. Slice avocados in half lengthwise. Remove pits.
2. Combine juice of 1 lime plus 1 Tbsp olive oil and coat avocados for grilling. Save remainder.
3. In small bowl, combine remaining lime juice and olive oil, plus another 1 Tbsp olive oil and juice from 1 more lime, hot sauce, onion, tomato, cilantro, and salt and pepper to taste.
4. Pre-heat grill to medium heat.
5. Combine first 8 ingredients in small bowl.
6. Skewer shrimp (soak wood skewers in water for about 1/2 hour before grilling).
7. Sprinkle seasoning over shrimp and drizzle with olive oil.
8. Place avocado and shrimp on the grill. Grill avocado for a few minutes or until you get nice grill marks.
9. Cook shrimp for about 3 minutes each side until pink.
10. Remove avocados and shrimp from heat.
11. Remove shrimp from skewers and lightly chop shrimp. Combine with salsa mixture.
12. Place a spoonful or two of salsa mixture in each avocado.
13. Enjoy the extra shrimp on the side with your avocado.
14. Serve as a side dish or appetizer.

# Vanessa Barajas
SAN DIEGO, CA

I've always loved food, but until about a year ago I hated cooking it. And, honestly, I sucked at it. In my head, though I was a master chef, whirling around my beautiful copper-pot-lined French kitchen, baking and sautéing to perfection impossible entrées over my mammoth Viking range, humming and chopping away so elegantly that even Julia Child would be envious. But, in reality, I was red in the face, frustrated, sweaty, with hair flying every which direction, smudges of ingredients everywhere, all over my face, clothes and not to mention the smallest of counter space in my tiniest of inglorious, non-French kitchens, trying to cook on that left burner, the crooked one that tilts, and is that something burning I smell?

My sad cooking journey could have ended here. It probably should have, but I'm just too stubborn.

I began my Paleo journey in September 2012 as part of a Whole 30 challenge with my CrossFit box. As most of you Paleo-ites know, you have to take an active role in planning and preparing your meals or it's just not going to work. I started slowly, mostly by "pinning" recipes on Pinterest and reading the who's-who of Paleo blogs. I also made a commitment to myself that I would try one new recipe a week. Slowly but surely, I found what worked and what didn't. I was so proud of myself and my creations on these momentous occasions that I started taking pictures of them and posting them on my Facebook and Instagram pages. My poor friends.

But they love me, so they pushed me to start a blog (to save themselves and all humanity!). My boyfriend, Brad, also thinks it's a great idea since he is usually my taste-testing guinea pig. I call him "my non-Paleo taste buds," and I figure if it tastes good to him, it probably legitimately tastes good! He's the Stewart to my Martha.

Hey, I just met you. And this is crazy. But here's my blog. So read it, maybe?
www.CleanEatingWithaDirtyMind.com

# Paleo Chocolate Pecan and Praline Cookies

Estimated Prep Time: 10 to 15 minutes
Estimated Cooking Time: 12 to 14 minutes
Servings: 18

2 cups sifted almond meal
1/2 cup unsweetened cocoa powder
1/2 tsp baking soda
1/4 tsp sea salt
1 cup chocolate chips
1/2 cup chopped pecans
2 organic cage-free eggs
1/3 heaping cup Chocolate Hazelnut Brownie
  Nikki's Coconut Butter (softened)
1/4 cup raw honey (liquid)
2 Tbsp coconut oil (liquid)
1/2 tsp vanilla extract

**Praline and chocolate topping ingredients:**
1/4 cup chopped pecans (crushed)
4 heaping Tbsp Macadamia Nut Cookie
  Nikki's Coconut Butter (softened)
4 Tbsp coconut crystals
1/2 tsp vanilla extract
Pinch sea salt
1 cup chocolate chips (for chocolate drizzle)

1. Make the chocolate pecan cookies first. While they're baking, prepare your praline topping.
2. Preheat oven to 350°F.
3. Line a baking sheet with parchment paper.
4. In a large bowl, mix the dry ingredients (almond meal, unsweetened cocoa powder, baking soda, and salt) thoroughly with a fork.
5. Add the chocolate chips and chopped pecans to the dry mixture and stir evenly.
6. In a separate bowl, mix the wet ingredients (eggs, softened Chocolate Hazelnut Brownie Nikki's Coconut Butter, honey, coconut oil, and vanilla extract).
7. Make a crater in the center of your dry mix and pour the wet ingredients into it. Stir the wet ingredients into the dry until evenly mixed.
8. Let dough chill in the fridge for at least 30 minutes.
9. Once your dough is ready, make medium-sized cookie-shaped balls with the palm of your hand. The dough won't spread while cooking so the shape you make them will be their final shape. Place on the parchment-lined baking sheet.
10. Bake for 12 to 14 minutes or until a toothpick comes out clean.
11. To make the pralines, crush the 1/4 cup of chopped pecans.
12. Place your crushed pecans in a medium-sized bowl. Add the pinch of salt, then the softened Macadamia Nut Cookie Nikki's Coconut Butter, coconut crystals, and vanilla extract. Mix until combined.
13. Now toast the pecan mixture in a pan over medium heat, constantly moving and flipping them with a spatula so they don't burn) until they're a toasty golden brown. They will smell incredible and then you'll know they're done (about 10 minutes).
14. Once the cookies are finished baking, let them cool. Then transfer the cookies onto a sheet of parchment paper to add the praline and chocolate toppings.
15. Melt your chocolate using the double-boiler method. Transfer the melted chocolate to a piping bag with desired tip (or my cheapskate way, a Ziploc baggie with a hole cut in the corner), and drizzle the chocolate over the cookies.
16. While the chocolate is still wet, crumble some pralines over the top of the cookie into the wet chocolate. Then add another layer of chocolate drizzle to set the pralines. Let harden and enjoy!

# Wendy Massa

ORLAND, CA

I have enjoyed a Paleo lifestyle for several years now. I first learned of the Paleo diet while training with Paleo guru Robb Wolf at his gym in Chico, California, in 2006. To say that Paleo has had a profound effect on my life is a bit of an understatement. In addition to the myriad health benefits I've experienced since going to a Paleo lifestyle (including energy, strength, and restful sleep, among other things), I even quit my job and began an entirely new business to help others enjoy the benefits of a Paleo lifestyle!

I realized early during my transition to a primal diet that healthy foods without harmful chemicals or additives were increasingly difficult to find near my home in rural northern California. So, with the help of my husband, Duane, we began raising our own hormone- and antibiotic-free grass-fed beef! At first, we were just raising grass-fed cattle for our own consumption, but following numerous requests and words of encouragement from friends, we decided to open Massa Natural Meats and produce enough grass-fed beef for all who wish to enjoy the health benefits that pasture-raised animals can provide.

The business keeps me, Duane, and our son, Hayden, quite busy, but eating Paleo, along with the physical work involved in running a small farm, keeps all of us in excellent health. In fact, during my pregnancy with Hayden, I adhered to a strict Paleo diet, despite my doctor's numerous concerns. When the results from the first standard round of maternal blood tests came in, my open-minded but skeptical doctor exclaimed, "Wendy, your blood work looks better than a non-pregnant woman half your age! Keep doing whatever it is you're doing."

Most days, we can be found working on our small farm, and we love to share our products and experiences with others. Drop us a message if you like! You'll find contact information as well as our all-natural, hormone- and antibiotic-free beef and lamb online at: www.MassaNaturalMeats.com.

# Paleo Broccoli Beef

Estimated Prep Time: 30 minutes
Estimated Cooking Time: 15 minutes
Servings: 4

My husband and I have enjoyed a 100-percent Paleo lifestyle for several years now. As many people ask, it's true that we occasionally miss some of our old favorites. **I LIKE TO TAKE THESE REMINISCENT CRAVINGS AS A CHALLENGE AND INSPIRATION TO CREATE NEW PALEO-FRIENDLY RECIPES.**

One cuisine we have missed is Chinese food. The use of soy and MSG in Chinese cooking had pretty much eliminated this food from our diet. Then I made a discovery... One afternoon while perusing the aisles of my favorite health food store, I came across coconut aminos.

With this discovery came a recipe that has since become a family favorite. I love to make it using our own grass-fed stir-fry beef. I hope you enjoy it!

2 lbs grass-fed fajita/stir-fry beef
1/2 cup extra-virgin olive oil
1 cup coconut aminos
1/4 tsp cayenne
1/4 tsp ginger
1 tsp sea salt
1 large red onion, chopped into
  1/2" pieces
1 Tbsp chopped garlic
4 cups broccoli florets

1. In a large bowl add olive oil, coconut aminos, cayenne, ginger, sea salt, beef, garlic, and red onion. Mix until beef and broccoli are well coated. Cover and let stand for 30 minutes.
2. In a large skillet or wok (I use a 12" skillet with lid), bring the beef mixture to a simmer on low-medium heat. Cook for about 5 minutes* until beef is just cooked; a little pink in the center is good. Don't overcook or cook too hot, or your meat will be dry and tough. With a slotted spoon, remove beef and set aside in a bowl, leaving juices in the pan.
3. Add broccoli to skillet and stir so that broccoli is well coated with the juices. Cover and cook, stirring occasionally until broccoli reaches desired tenderness, approximately 10 minutes.
4. Add beef and onion back to pan, mix, and heat for 1 minute. Serve.

*If you're using grain-fed beef or cutting your own stir-fry meat, cooking times may vary.

# Aglaée Jacob, MS, RD

TORONTO, CANADA

As a conventionally trained registered dietitian who stumbled upon the Paleo diet in 2010, it took a lot of research to convince me that eating more red meat and saturated fat and letting go of my soy and whole grains wouldn't kill me. My husband, Jonathan, and I had been eating the way I was taught was the healthiest, but I started having doubts after struggling with my weight and my health.

Paleo was the extreme opposite of everything I had learned, but I gathered enough evidence-based information to make me feel comfortable making the switch. My husband, always interested in maximizing his health and longevity (cancer runs on both sides of his family), jumped on the bandwagon at the same time.

We never looked back. Applying the principles of the Paleo diet helped us both take our health to the next level. Jonathan's anemia disappeared (anemia is uncommon in young males, but can be the consequence of a low-iron, high-phytate vegetarian diet) and his GERD (acid reflux) became easier to control. It helped me manage my digestive issues, regularize my hormones (PCOS) and blood sugar levels, and significantly improve my energy and cognitive function.

I was hooked and, despite fearing losing my dietitian license for telling my clients to replace skim milk and whole-grain bread with cholesterol-loaded eggs, real meat (instead of soy-based imitations), and saturated-fat-rich coconut oil, I took the plunge and started practicing in a way that was in line with my new, evolved view of nutrition.

Eating Paleo also allowed Jonathan and me to enjoy our time traveling and living overseas in South America, Australia, and Europe in the past few years. Now we're back home in Canada where I'm currently pursuing a naturopathic medicine degree. I find that eating Paleo is really helping me focus and learn a lot better. I of course wish I had known what I know now when I first started studying nutrition, but I'm very grateful that I kept an open mind and decided to give it a try.

We sometimes wish we were still living in Australia or Europe, which are real paradises for Paleo eaters due to their unrivaled food quality, but we know better than anyone that it's possible to find high-quality ingredients wherever you are. We now feel at home in Toronto, where we regularly participate in cow shares and get a weekly CSA organic vegetable basket.

www.Paleo-Dietitian.com

# Clean Chocolate

Estimated Prep Time: 15 minutes
Estimated Setting Time: 2 hours
Servings: 4-6

1/2 cup virgin coconut oil, grass-fed butter,
   or organic cocoa butter
2-4 Tbsp cocoa powder, unsweetened and organic
1 Tbsp organic coconut palm sugar or maple syrup
1/4-1/2 cup unsweetened dried coconut, nuts, and/or
   dried fruits (optional)
A few drops organic vanilla extract (optional)

1. Melt your chosen fat (coconut oil, butter, and/or
   cacao butter) in a small pot on low. Once melted,
   mix with the cacao powder and sweetener. The
   more cacao you add, the darker your homemade
   chocolate will be.
2. If you want to make two different varieties of your
   clean chocolate, separate chocolate mixture into
   two separate containers.
3. Add optional ingredients, such as half the
   chocolate with raisins and almonds and the other
   half with coconut and vanilla.
4. Pour chocolate mixture into silicon muffin molds,
   parchment paper or any other mold of your choice
   (grease it with coconut oil first to prevent sticking).
5. Put in the fridge for 1 to 2 hours to set.
6. Keep in mind that your chocolate will be more
   prone to melting than chocolate found at the store.
   Keep it in the fridge or freezer in a hermetic
   container until you're ready to eat it... if it lasts
   that long!

# Brittanie Duncan
AUSTIN, TX

I taught myself to cook four years ago after graduating from NYU's studio art program and moving to Lexington, Virginia. I'm passionate about art, health, fitness, and food. I fell in love with cooking and it has taken over as my primary creative outlet. I love learning new techniques and flavors to apply to my cooking.

My daily challenge, since going Paleo, is finding a healthy way to feed myself and my family without being a short-order cook. I used to make three separate dinners, but that was expensive, time-consuming, and frustrating. "Three Diets One Dinner" (www.ThreeDietsOneDinner.com) is my solution to this dilemma. This blog provides you with healthy, inspired Paleo recipes the whole family can enjoy. Occasionally I will throw in a tip or trick on sneaking vegetables in your meals.

Living Paleo in a non-Paleo family is possible. I took Concerta for nine years, but the whole time it was masking a hypothyroid condition. When I stopped taking it, I literally fell asleep. I had digestive issues, and chronic fatigue, which turned into depression. I visited many doctors, one who put me back on Concerta, one who put me on antidepressants, and one who put me on a thyroid replacement. None of those things solved my exhaustion, and I struggled to keep my weight down.

Last summer, I was saved by changing to a Paleo diet. It sounds crazy, but after a yearlong rollercoaster of trying to improve my health, this was it. Not only did Paleo improve my weight, energy, mood, and digestion, but I feel younger and stronger than ever. I now only eat meat, fish, poultry, vegetables, nuts, seeds, healthy fats (such as avocado and coconut oil), and a little fruit. I will occasionally eat goat cheese, and I do drink wine and clear liquor. I've eliminated anything processed or containing gluten, dairy, grains, soy, sugar, and legumes.

I also haven't been sick at all since I started Paleo. I was attracted to this diet and lifestyle because of the research demonstrating the dangers of processed foods and the diseases they cause, including cancer, diabetes, obesity, depression, Alzheimer's, autism, acne, thyroid problems, and digestive issues—and the list goes on.

So now my personal health philosophy goes something like this: Fix your body with food, fitness, and good sleep—not pills. Anyway, that's my story and I'm sticking with it. I feel great!

# Spicy Avocado Dressing

Estimated Prep Time: 5 minutes
Estimated Cooking Time: 5 minutes
Servings: 2 to 4

1/4 avocado
1 jalapeño
1 Tbsp minced onion
1 garlic clove
1/4 tsp cumin
Handful cilantro
2 Tbsp lemon or lime juice
2 Tbsp water
1-1/2 Tbsp champagne or white wine vinegar
1/2 tsp salt
1/2 tsp pepper

1. Combine all the ingredients in a blender.
2. Toss in a salad or use as a dip!

Full of flavor and nutrients, this dressing is a unique crowd pleaser. **THIS RECIPE CAME ABOUT WHEN I WAS CRAVING A LITTLE KICK FROM MY SALAD DRESSING** but also wanted to create something that was versatile enough to use as a dip.

## Chris Jax

NORTH YORK, CANADA

When I was an adolescent, I was always skinny despite being alternately active and sedentary, and eating what and when I wanted. Like many children, my metabolism was high and, in my 40s now, still seems to be high. I can still eat what I want without gaining weight. I have no doubt my genetic makeup has played a role in this, as my family is generally long and lean.

From teenage years into my late 20s, I competed in boxing. My training helped keep my 6'1" frame at a lean 165 pounds. However, my first romance was still food, so much that I became an apprentice in the food industry and completed my culinary training in Ontario in 1995. There I wrote my

ticket and worked as a fine-dining chef. A career transition began in 1998 when I joined the Canadian Forces, where I continued to stay fit. About this time, I retired from boxing and turned to a mix of weight training and cardio, and as a result I bulked up to a still-healthy-and-lean 185 pounds.

In 2008, some of my military co-workers introduced me to the sport of CrossFit. CrossFit gave me back the high-intensity workout I missed from my boxing days. I was hooked! Three years later, I attended and completed a certification course for CrossFit Level 1 Trainers (CFL1). The instructors were excellent and the course was well structured and informative. But when we reached the nutrition section, what I thought I knew about grains conflicted with their doctrine, and I found myself in complete disagreement (and irritation) with the claims they made about "bad" carbs and leaky gut.

I decided to do more research, however, and eventually shifted my conventional way of thinking. In the process, my family and I started to adopt the Paleo lifestyle and I now blog about it at www.ChristianJax.ca.

Stay primal!

**PAD THAI HAS ALWAYS BEEN A FAVORITE DISH OF MINE,** but going Paleo meant no peanuts and no noodles, so I had to come up with a Paleo version. The spiciness of the chili combined with the flavor of the almond butter makes this protein-rich dish a favorite in my household. Depending on your personal preference, you might need to adjust the heat level. This is one of the recipes I have posted on my blog at **www.Primalcut.wordpress.com.** Enjoy!

# Ultimate Paleo Pad Thai

Estimated Prep Time: 15 minutes
Estimated Cooking Time: 20 minutes
Servings: 4

3 Tbsp coconut oil
4 zucchini
1 chicken breast (boneless & skinless)
1 lb shrimp
1 egg
1 carrot, shredded (optional)
1 onion, diced
4 garlic cloves, minced
2 Tbsp ginger, fresh & minced
3 Tbsp almond butter
1 Tbsp apple cider vinegar
1 Tbsp fish sauce
2 Tbsp chili garlic sauce
2 limes (1 for garnish)
12 Thai basil leaves, julienne
Salt and pepper
Handful almonds, chopped
12 grape tomatoes, halved (optional)

1. Slice your zucchini thin to form long noodle strands (a mandoline is an excellent tool for this type of work).
2. Chop chicken into 1/4-inch pieces.
3. Mix together almond butter, cider vinegar, fish sauce, chili sauce and juice of 1 lime.
4. Scramble egg in a bowl and place to the side.
5. In a large frying pan, sauté onions in coconut oil over medium heat (have an extra frying pan and a colander at the ready).
6. Brown chicken in onions, followed closely with garlic and ginger.
7. Add almond butter mix and carrots (optional).
8. Turn heat up to medium-high and toss in zucchini and shrimp, which will take 5 to 10 minutes. Shrimp will turn pink and start to curl and zucchini should be al dente.
9. In second pan, cook egg omelet style, remove from pan, and keep pan ready with colander.
10. Strain zucchini over the second pan.
11. Add tomatoes and basil to the liquid and reduce over high heat.
12. Slice up egg and mix with zucchini and reduced liquid.
13. Garnish with almonds and a lime wedge.
14. Season with salt and pepper.

# Daphne Fong
## SAN JOSE, CA

It's incredible how much better I feel overall since going Paleo. In my family, I'm the one who's been affected the most by switching to Paleo in that I was born with autoimmune issues. This lifestyle has made a big difference in my skin and the crazy seasonal allergies that used to incapacitate me for a day or two are history. Although I still have itchy patches from my genetically inherited eczema, my skin has never looked or felt better.

Just the fact I feel energized and don't get as sluggish anymore makes me more excited about doing things with my young boys as a family—about being active and enjoying the outdoors whenever and wherever possible!

Now, instead of relying on instant noodles or prepackaged frozen foods, our meals are fresh and wholesome. I've learned to use spices and utilize different methods of cooking, and to be brave and try cooking with unfamiliar vegetables. Because we're also no longer eating rice or noodles with our meals, we've replaced them with more servings of vegetables. My kids are great eaters and are energetic without being overly rambunctious.

As a whole, going Paleo has made us all feel clear headed and energized!

I GOT THE BASIS OF THIS RECIPE from the March issue of Bon Appétit magazine. I've had to fiddle with a few things here and there—because I forgot details of the recipe or I didn't have the time or desire to obtain so many different spices and herbs. Instead of rice, I serve this with spaghetti squash.

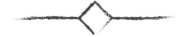

# Chicken and Sausage Jambalaya

Estimated Prep Time: 30 minutes
Estimated Cooking Time: 2 hours
Servings: 8

12 oz applewood smoked bacon, diced
1-1/2 lb smoked, fully cooked sausage (e.g., linguica),
  halved lengthwise and cut cross-wise into 1/2"-thick semicircle
1 lb andouille sausage, quartered lengthwise, cut cross-wise into
  1/2" cubes
1-1/2 lb onions, chopped (4-5 cups)
2 large celery stalks, chopped
1 (8- to 10-oz) red bell pepper, coarsely chopped
1 (8- to 10-oz) green bell pepper, coarsely chopped
6 large boneless, skinless chicken thighs, cut into 1-to-
  1-1/2"-thick pieces
4-5 Tbsp of Cajun seasoning
2 (14.5-oz) cans diced tomatoes with green chilies
2 cups low-sodium beef broth
8 green onions, chopped

1. Cook bacon in very large pot over medium-high
   heat until brown (but not yet crisp), stirring often
   (about 8 to 10 minutes).
2. Add smoked sausage and andouille and sauté until meat
   starts to brown in spots (about 10 minutes).
3. Add onions, celery, and bell peppers. Cook until vegetables
   start to soften, stirring occasionally.
4. Mix in chicken and cook until outside of chicken turns white,
   stirring often.
5. Stir in Cajun seasoning and let cook for another minute.
6. Add diced tomatoes and beef broth and stir to blend well.
   Add more cayenne (or Cajun seasoning) if desired.
7. Bring jambalaya to a boil.
8. Position rack in bottom third of oven and place pot in
   oven for about 45 minutes.
9. Garnish with some chopped green onions
   (maybe even some cilantro!).
10. Serve and enjoy!

# Elana Amsterdam

### BOULDER, CO

I was diagnosed with celiac disease in 1998. After three years on a strict gluten-free diet, I still suffered from digestive distress, so I decided to go grain free. I found immediate relief from this choice and have been on a grain-free eating plan ever since. This way of life is not all that challenging for me as I have no interest in going back to eating grains. Why would I want to eat something that makes me feel sick?

In addition to the foods I choose to put in my body, I find that proper rest and exercise are wonderful ways to enhance a healthy lifestyle. I sleep in a darkened room for a minimum of eight hours per night and engage in daily moderate exercise. I love walking and do a lot of gentle stretching, t'ai chi, Pilates, and very light weightlifting.

I had thought that some of my habits were a little odd (sleeping in a dark room with tin foil on the windows, anyone?), until I learned that there was a name for all of these seemingly disparate strategies: Paleo. After reading Dr. Loren Cordain's books, as well as Robb Wolf's, I realized that I had stumbled upon the grandfather and father of the Paleo movement, a movement of which I am so happy to be a part. I'm also a huge fan of Mark Sisson's work, as well as Diane Sanfilippo's. Thanks to the four aforementioned authors, and my reading of the medical literature and scientific studies, I'm learning more about how to live better every day.

www.ElanasPantry.com

# Brownies

Estimated Prep Time: 10 minutes
Estimated Cooking Time: 20 minutes
Servings: 16

1 cup blanched almond flour
1/4 tsp Celtic sea salt
1/4 tsp baking soda
4 oz baking chocolate (100% cacao)
7 Medjool dates (1/2-2/3 cup), pits removed
3 large eggs
1/2 cup coconut oil, melted
1/2 tsp vanilla stevia

1. In a food processor, pulse together almond flour, salt, and baking soda.
2. Pulse in squares of dark chocolate until texture is like coarse sand.
3. Pulse in dates until the texture of coarse sand.
4. Pulse in eggs.
5. Pulse in coconut oil and stevia until mixture is smooth.
6. Transfer mixture to a greased 8" x 8" baking dish.
7. Mixture will be very thick, so smooth with a spatula.
8. Bake at 350°F for 18 to 22 minutes.
9. Cool for 2 hours, then serve.

PHOTOGRAPHY ELANA AMSTERDAM

# Holly Gary

HOUSTON, TX

My Paleo journey began in 2012 shortly after returning from my honeymoon. I had heard about the "caveman" diet but didn't learn the specifics until joining CrossFit that spring. I've struggled with weight loss my entire life, not having been blessed with the speedy metabolism of my brothers. Health and longevity are truly important to me and fad diets and pills just aren't for me.

I listened to and read anything I could get my hands on... Robb Wolf's book and podcast, Balanced Bites, Primal Blueprint, you name it. For the first time, I believed in what I was doing to support my health and wellness. My friends and family were consistently hearing about the gut-brain barrier, autoimmunity, and carb replacement. It's like I was a junior scientist!

I lost my honeymoon weight and was feeling amazing. Each meal was satisfying and delicious, leaving me full until the next one. I had tons of energy and even got my husband on board. But things stalled. I engaged the advice of a doc in the Paleo Physicians Network and discovered I'm estrogen dominant and was experiencing adrenal fatigue, which I'm working to improve.

I was so enamored with Paleo and its promise of longevity and energy that I started a recipe website at www.PaleoAmore.com, which has been so successful! Mastering culinary creations has been a pastime of mine since the days my best friend and I recorded and watched every cooking show on the Food Network. I love making beautifully delicious meals and creating new recipes. My friends were surprised with what I can do with just meat and veggies.

My grandfather used to say, "Holly, do you eat to live or live to eat?" Now, I can comfortably say, "Both!"

# Costa Rican Ceviche

Estimated Prep Time: 10 minutes
Estimated Cooking Time: 2 hours
Servings: 6

2 tilapia filets (or any white fish)
1/2 lb shrimp
6 limes
4 lemons
1 tsp honey
2/3 cup coconut milk
1 cup tomato, finely chopped
1/2 red onion, finely chopped
1 cup avocado chunks
1/2 mango, chopped
Salt and pepper

1. Squeeze limes and lemons into a large, flat-bottomed bowl. Whisk in honey.
2. Slice tilapia into inch-size cubes and cut shrimp in thirds. Place in lemon/lime juice.
3. Pack tilapia and shrimp into the bowl and make sure juice covers it completely.
4. Place chopped tomatoes and red onion on top of fish, but don't mix.
5. Cover and chill for at least 2 hours. Fish should turn solid white.
6. Remove from fridge. Stir mixture so tomatoes and red onion are well incorporated.
7. Add coconut milk, avocado, and mango. Mix well.
8. Add salt and pepper to taste.
9. Enjoy!

My husband and I were traveling in Costa Rica on our honeymoon. **ONE OF THE BEST PALEO-FRIENDLY DISHES WE HAD THERE WAS THE CEVICHE.** It was light and fresh with a hint of sweetness. I tinkered with many recipes before finally creating this one. It brings us back to the beach every time we eat it!

# Karen Sorenson

LADSON, SC

I started the Paleo diet to help me reach my goal of losing 100 pounds and to get healthy before I started having kids of my own. It has turned into so much more than just a diet!  The Paleo lifestyle has showed me just how important it is to feed your body real food and what a powerful tool food can be in healing from years of poor diet and lifestyle. I no longer shop at the grocery store, filling my cart with boxes of processed food. Instead I frequent farmers markets with access to fresh, seasonal produce and local pastured meats and eggs. I now understand the importance of food quality and how it can have a major effect on my quality of life down the road.

In addition to food, Paleo is a lifestyle that has taught me the importance of taking care of myself and my environment. It has taught me to get out and soak up some Vitamin D while enjoying my surroundings. I have also come to understand that there is no time like the present to start making small changes that add up and make a huge impact on your life. It's not just a fad, but a lifestyle. The lessons I've learned with the Paleo lifestyle are powerful ones that I can pass on to my future children and help avoid passing on my family's heritage of obesity and diabetes.

# Ground Beef Skillet

Estimated Prep Time: 10 minutes
Estimated Cooking Time: 20 minutes
Servings: 4

1 lb ground beef
16 oz radishes, quartered
5 oz carrots, diced
3 cups spinach
3 Tbsp Dijon mustard
Salt, pepper, and granulated garlic to taste

I'm always looking for a **QUICK WEEKNIGHT MEAL THAT'S PACKED WITH LOTS OF VEGGIES.** This is easy to throw together and makes a delicious one-pan dish. www.LCOneDay.blogspot.com

1. Heat 1 to 2 Tbsp of oil in a large skillet over medium-high heat.
2. Add radishes and carrots and season with salt, pepper, and garlic to taste.
3. Sauté for 5 to 6 minutes or until veggies are halfway tender.
4. Push veggies to the sides of the pan and add ground beef to the middle.
5. Brown ground beef until cooked through. Drain excess fat and combine meat with veggies.
6. Add spinach and Dijon mustard.
7. Stir to combine and cook until spinach has wilted and veggies are tender (cover the pan if necessary to soften veggies).

I came into the world of Paleo about a year ago. It was a progression of steps that got me to where I am now, which started back in 2011. I started off by following a program for quitting sugar, and I felt so great afterward that I wanted to take things further. I then heard about the Whole30 program run by Melissa and Dallas Hartwig of whole9life.com, read their book *It Starts With Food*, and decided to give their 30-day challenge a go! I felt so much better afterward that I decided to continue on with a Paleo lifestyle. Of course, I'm only human, so I can't say that I'm 100-percent Paleo all of the time!

Since I started following Paleo, I have a lot more energy. I can go through a day without feeling like I need to take a nap or hitting the big afternoon energy slump that I used to. I can also get through the day without having to snack constantly because the food that I eat now doesn't leave me feeling hungry an hour later. I've also noticed improvements in my hair and skin, as well as in my sleep, and I'm more in tune with my body: If I notice any difference in my skin, hair, or even digestion, I know it's time to look back on what I've been eating. If I'm lacking energy or find it hard to exercise, I know to examine my sleep or stress.

Even though my husband isn't Paleo, he still eats the foods I cook, and we both make sure to buy the best-quality foods we can afford and stay away from processed or boxed foods. We both enjoy cooking, so having fresh ingredients on hand means we know exactly what goes into the food we cook. Of course, we still eat out occasionally, but when we do we try to make the best possible choices from what's available.

The Paleo lifestyle to me is not a one-size-fits-all approach, but more about getting to know YOUR body and what works for you. I look at it as a foundation upon which to build, kind of like a house: You have the base, and what you build on top of it is up to you—and you can make modifications to it along the way to best suit your needs.

My background is Persian, and lamb is something I grew up eating. MY MUM WOULD OFTEN MAKE LAMB IN THE SLOW COOKER FOR US, AND I REMEMBER IT BEING SO DELICIOUS AND MELT-IN-YOUR-MOUTH TENDER. Having moved to the U.S. recently from Australia and missing my mum's cooking, I decided to recreate this childhood favorite. The smell from the slow cooker when making this meal reminds me of her and of home. I serve this with cauliflower mash since it's traditionally served with rice.

# Persian Slow Cooker Lamb

Estimated Prep Time: 20 minutes
Estimated Cooking Time: 6-8 hours
Servings: 4 to 5

3 lb grass-fed lamb shanks
1 onion
1 medium sweet potato, peeled
  and diced into chunks
1 large red bell pepper, de-seeded
  and diced
1 large portobello mushroom, diced
1-2 Tbsp ghee
2-3 Tbsp Advieh spice blend
  (Persian spice mix, which is a blend of
  1 tsp ground cinnamon, 1 tsp ground
  nutmeg, 1 tsp ground cardamom, and
  1/2 tsp ground cumin)
2 Tbsp saffron water (a pinch of saffron
  threads dissolved in 1/4 cup boiling water)
1 head of garlic, cloves peeled and
  left whole
2 (14.5-oz) cans diced tomatoes
1 Tbsp tomato paste
Sea salt and freshly cracked black
  pepper to taste
Water

1. Remove lamb shanks from the fridge and allow to come to room temperature.
2. Make saffron water by boiling 1/4 cup water and stirring in a pinch of saffron threads. Set aside.
3. Heat 1-2 Tbsp ghee in a large non-stick skillet over medium heat. In the meantime, slice the onions into half-moons. Cook onions until just softened.
4. While onions are cooking, season lamb shanks with sea salt and freshly cracked black pepper on all sides.
5. Remove onions from the skillet onto a heatproof plate.
6. Sear the lamb shanks in batches in the skillet for 2-3 minutes per side. Remove lamb shanks and place on a heatproof dish.
7. Add onions back to the skillet, then add Advieh spice blend. On medium heat, stir onions and spices until you can smell the spices (about a minute).
8. Turn off heat and place onion and spice mixture into the bottom of a slow cooker/crock pot.
9. Add sweet potato, red bell pepper and mushroom on top of onions.
10. Place lamb shanks on top of vegetables. Pour over the canned diced tomatoes and tomato paste.
11. Add saffron water and stir to combine.
12. Place garlic cloves into the sauce, distributing them evenly. Season with salt and pepper.
13. If the liquid level in the slow cooker/crock pot looks too low, add some filtered water about a 1/4 cup at a time. Remember the liquid level in the slow cooker will remain the same throughout the cooking process.
14. Cover the slow cooker/crock pot and cook on low for 6 to 8 hours or until lamb is done.
15. Serve with cauliflower mash.

# Margaret Cordill

BLOOMINGTON, IL

The reasons that brought me to the Paleo lifestyle are not the same reasons I've stayed. The life I had before Paleo is not the same life that I am living now.

I started flirting with the Paleo lifestyle at the gentle urgings of my CrossFit "family" at my beloved box, the Body Compound. They explained to me the health benefits of Paleo, along with the promise of improved WOD times, a more efficient workout, and just generally looking and feeling better. It was difficult for me to accept the idea of rethinking much of what I had learned about healthy eating habits to that point. I had been diligently cooking "healthy" food for my family for years and doing just fine, or so I thought. In my mind, I was eating healthfully, so I thought I would focus on changing my diet just a bit to get those better WOD times and look better in my clothes. The important stuff. I ate fewer servings of grains and more vegetables, added red meats back into our diet sporadically, and bought some coconut oil to use on occasion. I was sure I could find the results I needed this way. Nope!

Through a stroke of luck I discovered that a new friend of mine had recently removed grains from her diet in hopes of eliminating the same symptoms I had been having for years. I had visited two gastroenterologists and neither of them ever suggested a change in my diet. I'm a little ashamed that I didn't immediately take more responsibility for my own health and do more research, but I trusted the doctors. After this revelation, though, I threw myself into Paleo. The results were drastic and life changing. My pain from bloating was gone, I lost weight and was able to maintain it, my feelings of depression gradually faded away, my head was clearer, I was able to stop taking Ritalin, my mood swings were down to normal, and I was actually happy. My husband and daughters are also feeling the benefits of Paleo in similar ways to what I have experienced.

Now I teach Paleo cooking classes so that I can pass on my positive experiences and help others. The way Paleo has changed my life is immeasurable, and I'm forever thankful.

# Red Pepper Dip

Estimated Prep Time: 10 minutes
Estimated Cooking Time: 25 minutes
Servings: 1-1/2 to 2 cups

6 red bell peppers, roasted, peeled and chopped
2/3 cup almond flour
1/3 cup raw walnuts, toasted and chopped
3 garlic cloves, minced
1/2 tsp salt
1 Tbsp fresh lemon juice or to taste
2 tsp raw honey
1 tsp ground cumin
1/2 tsp red pepper flakes
1/4 plus 2 Tbsp extra-virgin olive oil

This is a recipe I've used for years that I "converted" from a more traditional one when I started eating Paleo. It's widely loved by non-Paleo-ers too! **I OFTEN GET REQUESTS TO BRING IT TO PARTIES.** This dip is great to have on hand with raw veggies for a flavorful, satisfying snack. It's also wonderful with pork and chicken.

1. Preheat broiler.
2. Cut peppers in half lengthwise. Stem, seed, and devein. Place them skin side up on a broiler pan lined with parchment paper. Broil until completely blackened, 12 to 15 minutes.
3. Transfer peppers to a large bowl and cover with plastic wrap. Let cool for about 15 minutes. Remove blackened skin.
4. In a blender or food processor, combine peppers and all remaining ingredients except the oil.
5. With the machine running, gradually add the olive oil.
6. Serve with raw vegetables.

# Kelly Brozyna

BOULDER, CO

My husband, kids, and I are pretty much attached at the hip. We're obsessed with each other, for better or worse. I can't stand to be parted from them for very long. Of course, if you offered me a nice paid-for vacation with my sweetie, just the two of us, say, for a week in Bermuda, I would JUMP at the chance. In fact, forget Bermuda, it could be an hour's drive from my house and I'd be thrilled. But then I would come running right back, wanting to spend every second of the day with the munchkins. Even when they drive me up the wall. That's me.

Two of the biggest reasons why we homeschool the girls (we have three) is so that we can be together, and so that we can be outside. We like to get out and get dirty—hiking, biking, and just playing around. In the park, in the mountains, or at the beach: Life is good. An active outdoor lifestyle is as important to us as eating the kinds of foods our Paleo ancestors ate. And of course it's also important to recharge. We love to sleep in late, and get plenty of rest when we need it.

I have celiac disease, and my middle daughter, Ashley, is allergic to wheat. Removing all grains from our gluten-free diet took our wellbeing from pretty good to great. It improved our mental clarity, and eliminated the digestive problems we had still been having with gluten-free grains. Shortly after going dairy free, our skin cleared up, and my endometriosis was gone.

It's been about nine years now, and in all honesty, we don't miss gluten or dairy at all. We have never felt deprived without grains or dairy. I've made everything from ice cream to yogurt to sour cream—all with coconut, cashews, and hemp seeds.

You can find hundreds of free recipes on my blog, www.TheSpunkyCoconut.com, as well as in my cookbooks, *The Spunky Coconut Dairy-Free Ice Cream Cookbook* and *The Paleo Chocolate Lovers Cookbook*.

, Kelly

# Strawberry Rhubarb Pie

Estimated Prep Time: 20 minutes
Estimated Cooking Time: 22 minutes
Servings: 8

**Crust:**

1 cup almond flour

1/2 cup coconut flour, sifted to remove lumps

1/4 cup plus 2 Tbsp applesauce with no
 added sugar

1/4 cup melted coconut oil

3 Tbsp flax seed meal

1 Tbsp honey

1 Tbsp apple cider vinegar

1 tsp baking soda

**Filling:**

2-1/2 cups frozen rhubarb (do not thaw first)

2-1/2 cups frozen strawberries (do not thaw first)

1/2 cup coconut sugar

2 Tbsp arrowroot powder

2 tsp agar powder (not flakes)

1-1/2 tsp ground cinnamon

Pinch sea salt

1. Preheat oven to 350°F.
2. Whisk almond flour, coconut flour, flax seed meal, and baking soda in a bowl.
3. Mix applesauce, melted coconut oil, honey, and apple cider vinegar in a separate bowl.
4. Add dry ingredients to wet ingredients, and combine with an electric mixer.
5. Press crust into the pie dish and par-bake for 5 minutes. Set aside to cool.
6. Add frozen rhubarb, frozen strawberries, coconut sugar, cinnamon, and salt to a medium-sized pot.
7. Bring berries to a simmer, and simmer uncovered for about 15 minutes.
8. Whisk agar powder into the bubbling mixture so that it is well incorporated.
9. Turn off the heat and whisk arrowroot powder into the filling as well.
10. Add the filling to the crust and bake for 7 minutes.
11. Let the pie cool on the counter, then chill to set. Serve at room temperature with whipped coconut cream.

# Laura Russell
## PORTLAND, OR

Like many people, my journey to good health was a long one. Although both of my pregnancies were troublesome, the second one triggered a host of medical issues that were not only difficult to diagnose, but also became seemingly permanent fixtures in my post-partum life. I had chronic pelvic pain, numbness, overwhelming fatigue, dangerous levels of "brain fog," and eventually more serious symptoms like facial paralysis, tingling limbs, and confusion. Over the course of four years, I saw every type of specialist imaginable and no one could make sense of it. Eventually, I turned to a naturopathic physician with the simple hope of keeping my head above water, and she suggested trying an elimination diet.

Never for a moment did I consider that food could be the source of my problems, but as soon as gluten and dairy were out of my system, the symptoms promptly disappeared. I've been gluten free for six years now, and the positive changes in my life have been dramatic. I regained my health, my energy and, quite frankly, my sanity simply by feeding my body what it needs.

Recently, I've been tweaking my diet a bit more, gauging how I feel when I'm not eating grains, beans, or sugar. It's clear that I feel my best when I stick to eating simple meals filled with lean animal protein, healthy fats, and vegetables. As a result, my newfound energy has even led me to seek out new and interesting forms of exercise, something that had never crossed my mind in the past.

Some people view the way I eat as restrictive, but to them I say this: I have completely regained my health—no prescriptions, no procedures—simply by eliminating certain foods from my life. Is it worth it? To me it's a no-brainer.

www.LauraBRussell.com

# Roasted Halibut with Green Olive Relish

Estimated Prep Time: 15 minutes
Estimated Cooking Time: 15 minutes
Servings: 4

1 cup pitted and halved green olives, such as
   Cerignola, Lucque, or Picholine
1/2 cup packed parsley leaves
1 Tbsp drained capers
Grated zest of 1 orange (about 1 tsp)
2 Tbsp orange juice
3/4 tsp freshly ground black pepper
3 Tbsp plus 1 tsp olive oil
1-1/2 lb halibut fillet, about 1-1/2 inches thick
1/2 tsp salt

For a lovely presentation, cook one whole piece of halibut instead of individual portions. Top the fish with the olive relish and bring it to the table on a platter. Salad with a simple mustard vinaigrette makes a perfect accompaniment. **GRILLED HALIBUT, SALMON, PORK TENDERLOIN, OR ROASTED STURGEON TASTE EQUALLY DELICIOUS WITH THE RELISH.**

1. In a food processor, combine olives, parsley, capers, orange zest, orange juice, 1/2 tsp of the pepper, and 3 Tbsp olive oil. Pulse to a coarse puree.
2. Serve at room temperature. The relish will keep, tightly covered, in the refrigerator for up to 2 days.
3. Heat the oven to 450°F. Pat halibut dry and put it in a baking dish. Rub fish with remaining tsp of olive oil and sprinkle salt and remaining 1/4 tsp black pepper over the top.
4. Cook fish until there is a tiny bit of translucence remaining when you check with a knife, 12 to 15 minutes for 1-1/2-inch thick fillets. Take care not to overcook, as it will continue cooking as you bring it to the table.
5. Serve halibut topped with green olive relish.

# Mary Shenouda
SAN FRANCISCO, CA

There isn't a single part of my life that Paleo hasn't changed for the best, and it's still just the beginning. My story isn't much different from the many extraordinary journeys you've probably read about or perhaps even experienced firsthand. In 2011 I was confirmed as having not only celiac disease but also an intolerance to both casein and soy. How awesome is that? No sarcasm: Next to attending the World Series, this was the greatest day of my life. But the funny thing is I didn't know just how great. I believe I'm still far from the potential of my current journey.

Prior to being diagnosed, I went about life feeling very "sickly" for as long as I can remember. As I become a young woman, the things that had been labeled simply as "chronic syndromes" took on a more serious tone when my doctor hinted at "celiac." Sparing you details that would take a whole book to cover, I'll fast forward to the moment I decided to take matters into my own hands. With the help of EnteroLabs, I learned of my "celiac plus," and with some research landed upon the Paleo diet through Dr. Terry Wahls.

I immediately began to adjust my cooking style to fit into my mostly Paleo lifestyle, a change that proved to be physically and spiritually transformative. Every sickness disappeared and I had the epiphany that I had found my passion. Food has always been emotional for me; it's a vessel that allows me to connect with others. Regardless, I threw caution to the wind and decided to make a huge career change, going from a technology executive to a Paleo chef.

Within three months I had a full client list, and within six months I had a celebrity client list. Today, I'm cooking for professional athletes and collaborating with Michael Mina to bring the Paleo experience into the fine-dining world. There are many amazing educators in the Paleo community; my role is to translate their teachings onto the plate and bring those teachings to the world's mouths in the form of real, delicious food. And so, when it comes to how Paleo has changed my life... this is just the beginning.

# Bison "Sliders"

Estimated Prep Time: 45 minutes
Estimated Cooking Time: 1-1/2 hours
Servings: 10 to 15 sliders

1 lb ground bison
1 egg yolk
1 onion, medium sized
1/2 cup shallots
1 tomato
6 oz tomato paste
3 garlic cloves
4 (fat) sweet potatoes
1 calf's liver, chopped
Fresh figs
Cumin
Salt, pepper, chili flakes to taste

I'm a tech-sales junkie turned chef after a discovery of food intolerance to almost everything. **I WANTED TO SHOW MY FRIENDS THAT FOOD CAN STILL BE FUN AND DELICIOUS**—I also wanted to make liver in a palatable way so they'd give it a go. I made "be-livers" out of them! At first glance, you think these sliders really are on buns. I love that aesthetic trickery! What made me happier were the smiles on people's faces as they took their first bites and declared they now love liver.

1. Slice sweet potatoes into thick, bun-like slices. Sprinkle with a little salt and olive oil and lay them on a cookie sheet. Bake for 25 minutes at 350°F, until slightly soft. Remove but keep them on the cookie sheet for a broil session later.
2. Chop up onion, shallots, tomato and half of the garlic. Toss into saucepan and brown with olive oil until onions start to darken.
3. In a mixing bowl, knead the browned goodness into the ground bison, adding the egg yolk, tomato paste, pinch of cumin, and salt and pepper to taste.
4. On a cookie sheet, lay out your meat into mini patties. Bake at 350°F until your desired meat preference is achieved. Medium will take about 15 to 20 minutes.
5. In another sauce pan throw in the chopped figs with olive oil and heat until the figs are softened. Throw in the garlic, liver, and a little salt to taste, and fry it up until the garlic looks candied. Set aside for topping.
6. Broil sweet potato slices for 10 minutes to firm them up and give them a slight crunch so they hold together as buns. (Make sure you've removed your patties from the oven before you broil the "buns.")
7. Assemble your sliders. Add avocado for some cream to the bite. Eat with a smile.

# Katrina Barrilleaux
## LANCASTER, CA

Our family started off 2011 by introducing the Paleo lifestyle and CrossFit into our home after my husband had spent several hours researching ways to help our family become healthier. After a few weeks, we started noticing a difference in the way we looked and the way we felt. Our clothes fit looser, our oily skin normalized, migraine headaches disappeared, cramps and facial blemishes were gone, and we didn't have that foggy, tired feeling all the time.

Several weeks later, others started noticing a difference in the way we looked and how we seemed to have more energy. The children's teachers even commented on how the kids were more focused in class! My husband and I kept getting asked the same questions, so I started blogging (at www.ANewMe18.blogspot.com) about our transformation so others could get answers there and share their own experiences. That led to me starting a Paleo Recipe Exchange and Potluck (P.R.E.P.) several times a year where everyone would bring a Paleo recipe to share and try new dishes. The recipes would then be added to the blog so everyone could have access to them. We also posted information about where to find Paleo-friendly ingredients around town. The blog eventually led to a Paleo Facebook group where people could post their Paleo "finds," ask questions, and share recipes.

My family and I have enjoyed working out together, cooking together, and shopping at the local farmers markets!

# Applesauce Strawberry Omelet

Estimated Prep Time: 5 minutes
Estimated Cooking Time: 10 minutes
Servings: 1

3 large eggs
2 Tbsp unsweetened applesauce
2 or 3 fresh, organic strawberries, chopped
Dash cinnamon
Dash vanilla

The recipe came about because of my love of French toast. Whenever I made it, I would always make scrambled eggs with the leftover egg mixture. One day, I decided to make an omelet instead, and fell in love!

*This recipe originally appeared in the May/June 2011 issue of Paleo Magazine.*

1. While heating up a skillet, beat together eggs, cinnamon, and vanilla in a bowl.
2. Pour egg mixture into skillet. Cook until mostly set, then flip.
3. Spread applesauce and strawberries over half the omelet.
4. Fold in half and slide onto a plate. Enjoy!

# Kyle Roberts

### AUBURN, WA

For our family, Paleo didn't save our lives or anything. I wasn't diagnosed with any disease, but it did give us much improvement. My wife and I found the Paleo lifestyle when she found out she was pregnant with our first son. I was pushing 200 pounds and was extremely out of shape, and I didn't want our son to grow up with a father who couldn't run around the house or play sports with him.

I started working out at home and doing some research about going dairy free, since both of us found dairy was a slight problem for us. Around that time, I came across Mark's Daily Apple. It was great timing because Mark Sisson's first book, *The Primal Blueprint*, was about to come out. I read through his book, then Robb Wolf's *The Paleo Solution*, and the rest is history.

The transition was a little difficult, and my wife took it harder (I can't imagine transitioning to full-on Paleo during pregnancy). But she did her best and kept her grains to a minimum. I can still remember the last sandwich I ate. I hadn't had any grains for a few weeks, but all we had in the house was bread and tuna, so we made tuna sandwiches—and I felt horrible. I knew then that my body didn't like grains.

After that, the transition was pretty smooth. We feel lucky that we didn't have to transition our kids to Paleo. They have never known anything different. So I'm grateful that we found this healthy lifestyle when we did. Now we are all a healthy, lively family, and we owe it all to Paleo!

# Zucchini Pasta with Avocado Cream Sauce

Estimated Prep Time: 15 minutes
Estimated Cooking Time: 15 minutes
Servings: 2 to 4

4 small zucchini
2 Tbsp coconut oil
1 avocado
Juice of a half lemon
Salt and pepper
Handful fresh basil
2 Tbsp olive oil
3 Tbsp coconut milk (or more olive oil)
Olives (for topping)

1. Cut the zucchini into noodles. You can do this by hand or using a mandolin. Toss the zucchini with salt and set aside. (This will help it dry out a little.)
2. Chop olives and set aside.
3. In a food processor or blender, add avocado, lemon juice, olive oil, and coconut milk, and blend until creamy.
4. Add basil and more olive oil if needed.
5. Heat pan with coconut oil and toss in zucchini. Cook for just a few minutes over medium heat.
6. When the noodles are done, throw sauce into the pan while it's still a little hot and mix.
7. Serve topped with chopped olives and some pepper.

**WHO DOESN'T LOVE AVOCADO?** I can eat a few a day sometimes. I got the inspiration for this recipe from another recipe of mine for salmon patties with avocado cream sauce. I thought that by thinning out the sauce a little, it might go really well with noodles. And there you have it!

# Kimberly Brown
### STERLING, VA

My husband and I decided to give Paleo a try after hearing about it from our friends. We thought they were crazy and that Paleo could not be an eating style we could stick with. One day, though, Brandon decided it was worth a shot. We jumped right in three days before Thanksgiving and haven't regretted it for a moment. At first, it was hard knowing what to eat, what we can't eat, and what works for our bodies. But after three weeks, we both felt so good that we decided we would never go back to our old eating habits.

Before that, I had been having digestion issues and felt tired all the time. After several doctors' appointments and being prodded and probed, I got no answers. I had severe anxiety and panic attacks for which doctors gave me Xanax. After about three months of eating a clean Paleo diet, I no longer needed the medications and my body's digestion started working great! Brandon lost more than 60 pounds within six months, and gained health and fitness motivation. He used to suffer from migraines and stomach issues but since he cut out dairy, gluten, and sugar, he hasn't had any of those problems. He's also gone from a slightly active guy to a competitor. We've competed in several running races and a triathlon together, and he has gone on to be part of Thunderbird Energetica's racing team. With the team, he just completed his second half marathon. We enjoy being outside swimming, biking, hiking, and stand up paddle (SUP) boarding. You name it and we'll try it!

Recently, Brandon and I decided to bring a little one into the world, and I'm currently eight months pregnant. I've been Paleo through my pregnancy, and I've felt fantastic the whole time, with no morning sickness. The times that I've made poor choices, I noticed I would get heartburn or headaches. I have maintained a healthy weight, have a good amount of energy, and continue to grow a healthy little one.

We've seen so many changes in our lives because of how good we feel, and we both accredit that to our Paleo lifestyle.

# Sweet Apple Rabbit Skewers

Estimated Prep Time: 40 minutes
Estimated Cooking Time: 8 minutes
Servings: 7 large skewers

**Rabbit marinade ingredients:**
2 lb rabbit, cut into cubes
1/2 cup apple cider vinegar
1/2 tsp cinnamon
1/8 tsp cumin

**Apple marinade ingredients:**
1 Tbsp maple syrup
1/2 tsp Kerrygold butter, melted
1/8 tsp cinnamon
1 Granny Smith apple, cubed

**Basting ingredients:**
1 Tbsp maple syrup
1/2 tsp Kerrygold butter, melted
1/8 tsp cinnamon

1. Place water, vinegar, cumin and cinnamon in a large bowl.
2. Butcher and cube the rabbit, add to the bowl, and set aside for 30 minutes.
3. In a separate medium bowl, add syrup, cinnamon, and butter, and mix well.
4. Cube apple and add it to the medium bowl, and set aside for 10 minutes.
5. In a small dish, combine syrup, cinnamon, and butter for basting.
6. Preheat grill to about 300°F and brush grates with oil.
7. Assemble your skewers to your liking (e.g., rabbit, apple, rabbit, etc.) and brush lightly with basting mixture.
8. Grill skewers 4 minutes on each side, basting when you flip them over.
9. Enjoy!

**MY HUSBAND IS AN AVID HUNTER** and I'm usually open to trying new meats, especially since going Paleo last year. When we saw rabbit at a local farmers' market, my husband suggested we try it. I was initially not too thrilled with the idea, but he begged me to give it a chance, so we took some home. I spent two days planning and thinking about potential recipes, and this is what I came up with. After we enjoyed this meal, I gave my husband full permission to hunt rabbit so we can stock our fridge with this high-protein meat!

# Shanti Landon
NEWCASTLE, CA

The Paleo lifestyle was a lifesaver for my husband—and it improved the quality of life of the rest of my family so much that we all stuck with it! After being diagnosed with celiac disease, my husband found some relief by going gluten free, but it wasn't until he cut out all grains, dairy, sugar, and legumes that he noticed a dramatic improvement. It literally saved his life. He had been in awful pain for years, suffering from intestinal pain, uncomfortable bowel movements, mental anxiety, and many other unexplained illnesses. He couldn't believe how much better he felt once we changed our diet. He actually started to gain weight, after wasting away to 130 pounds at six feet tall. He's now 145 pounds (still skinny!) but feeling incredible.

Our son, who had suffered from severe allergies, asthma, and eczema, was also medicine free for the first time in his life. The joint pain I'd had for over 15 years, as well as my irregular periods, disappeared, and my mental fog was gone.

Our overall health improved in other ways, too, and we rarely get sick in the winter anymore. We are all more "stable" health-wise, and are full believers in the benefits of a Paleo lifestyle!

www.CleanEatsInTheZoo.com

# Paleo Pumpkin Bundt Cake with Coconut Cream Glaze

Estimated Prep Time: 15 minutes
Estimated Cooking Time: 40 to 50 minutes
Servings: 8 to 10

**For the cake:**
4 cups almond flour
1/2 tsp salt
1 tsp baking soda
1 Tbsp cinnamon
3/4 tsp allspice
1/2 tsp ground ginger
3 eggs
3/4 cup unsweetened, full-fat coconut milk
1 (15-oz) can pureed pumpkin
1 cup pure maple syrup
1 tsp vanilla

**For the glaze:**
1/2 cup coconut cream concentrate, melted
1 Tbsp coconut milk
3 Tbsp pure maple syrup
1/2 tsp pure vanilla extract
Water

This cake is so good, all of my taste testers raved about it.
**IT'LL WOW THE SOCKS OFF ANYONE WHO TRIES IT!**

1. Preheat oven to 340°F and grease a Bundt pan with coconut oil (very important!).
2. In a large bowl, combine dry ingredients.
3. In a separate bowl, whisk together eggs, coconut milk, pumpkin, maple syrup, and vanilla.
4. Combine dry and wet ingredients. Pour into greased pan and bake in oven for 40 to 50 minutes, or until inserted toothpick comes out clean.
5. Let cool for 30 minutes on a wire rack before turning upside down onto a serving platter.
6. While it cools for another 15 to 20 minutes, prepare the glaze.
7. After cake has cooled, drizzle glaze over it and store in fridge for best results.

**Glaze:**
Combine coconut cream, coconut milk, syrup, and vanilla in a bowl. It will thicken, so add water slowly until it reaches a "glaze" consistency.

# Michelle Norris
### KYLE, TX

I didn't come to the Paleo diet joyously, but kicking and screaming. My husband, Keith, had been Paleo for about a year when he finally convinced me that I had an issue with gluten. My specialty, as a chef, was Italian, making my own pasta and pizza dough, so this was not a happy revelation. However, three weeks into Paleo, all my post-meal stomach issues disappeared, along with my IBS, CFS, and fibromyalgia, and the dull, aching headaches I had daily. I also believed rheumatoid arthritis was causing my knee and lower-back pain. Poof! Gone.

While I still wasn't happy that I had to give up foods I loved just to be healthy, a few months later, some friends I hadn't seen in a while said I looked amazing and had clearly lost a lot of weight, and they asked me what I'd done. In my mind, I had done nothing but eat. That's when it finally hit me that this was information that should be shared. Today, Paleo is my life: I not only eat it, I live, breathe, and share it with thousands of people through my many Paleo businesses.

I am a self-taught, life-long gourmand, with a love for coaching others in the finer points of achieving true kitchen mojo. A burning desire to rewrite food policy on a national level as a "credentialed" food crusader has me currently pursuing a degree in culinary arts/nutrition. By creating new, innovative Paleo versions of avant-garde gourmet foods, I have won over even hardened skeptics to the idea that one need not sacrifice love of fabulous tasting food en route to achieving— and maintaining—true ancestral wellness. As my food philosophy, "Variety, flavors, and herbs are the spices of life," suggests, I experiment continually with an incredible home collection of exotic spices, herbs, vinegars, and oils to create an ever-expanding repertoire of amazing dishes.

www.TheRealPaleoFX.com

# Braised Bacon Brussels Sprouts

Estimated Prep Time: 15 minutes
Estimated Cooking Time: 25 minutes
Servings: 4

1 lb Brussels sprouts
6-8 slices applewood smoked bacon
2-3 Shallots
1 cup duck stock (chicken stock will also work)
1/3 cup balsamic vinegar
Fresh cracked pepper and sea salt

1. Slice shallots thinly and set them aside.
2. Render bacon in a large skillet over medium-high heat. Once bacon is done and crisp, pull it from the pan and place it on a few paper towels to drain. (Leave bacon oil/renderings in pan.)
3. While bacon is cooking, cut top stem area away from each Brussels sprout, slice it in two, and place the halves in a colander. Remove any yellowed or dead leaves. (Don't toss good leaves that have fallen off, though—throw them in, too!) Rinse well and shake to remove as much excess water as possible.
4. Add sliced shallots to hot pan and allow them to caramelize for a minute or two.
5. Add sprouts to pan, placing them cut side down. Cook for about 5 to 7 minutes to get them brown and crispy. If there's too many to put them all face down, simply toss the remaining ones on top and then after a few minutes, work those down to the bottom and turn over the ones you put in first.
6. After they've browned, stir sprouts to ensure they are all coated with the bacon oil and coat them with a nice amount of fresh cracked pepper and sea salt.
7. Turn the heat down to medium, add stock, cover the pan, and let sprouts simmer for about 15 minutes or until you can easily slide in a fork.
8. Sprinkle vinegar liberally over sprouts. Tear bacon into small pieces and sprinkle over sprouts.
9. Enjoy!

I loved sautéed cabbage but always feared Brussels sprouts growing up, hearing how awful they were. **BUT AS A RATIONAL ADULT, I THOUGHT, THEY LOOK LIKE TINY LITTLE CABBAGES, SO THEY CAN'T POSSIBLY BE BAD.** I decided to make them in a similar way to how I usually make cabbage (although I like cabbage a little crisp and don't usually braise it). But then I read that Brussels sprouts really should be braised to remove bitterness, and voila! My recipe was born from learning that braising, tenderness, and sautéing first can help those sprouts impart some great flavors.

# Michelle Trescott

SEATTLE, WA

After a decade of veganism, my husband and I decided to adopt a Paleo diet to help with my increasing health concerns. I had spent a year sick after a diagnosis of both Hashimoto's and celiac disease, when a gluten-free diet had done nothing to help my symptoms. In an act of desperation, we decided to ditch the grains and start eating meat—and we haven't looked back since. After making some additional restrictions for the Autoimmune Protocol (a version of Paleo that restricts eggs, dairy, nuts, seeds, and nightshades), I regained my health and was able to return to work and the activities I love.

In the transition, my husband discovered that he had a lot of grain-triggered digestive issues that were cleared up by going Paleo. He also found his performance as a cyclist improve by leaps and bounds, and he started to make gains in his training that he had been unable to achieve previously. Both of us have clearer, softer skin, sleep soundly, have less anxiety, and rarely get sick.

Besides having an incredible effect on our well-being, Paleo has encouraged us to live simply and more self sufficiently. Now we spend time outside, cultivating a garden and raising chickens, instead of being indoors watching TV. Gatherings with friends are focused on quality meals as well as sharing our food resources and knowledge with others. Developing relationships with the farmers who grow our food and raise the meat that we purchase has brought us a deeper sense of community, as well as made us feel more connected to the earth.

www.AutoImmune-Paleo.com

# Coconut Raspberry "Cheesecake"

Estimated Prep Time: 30 minutes
Estimated Cooking Time: 35 minutes (plus 12 hrs chill time)
Servings: 8

**Crust:**
3 cups pitted dates, soaked for
  5 minutes in warm water
1 cup coconut oil, melted
1/3 cup coconut flour
1/3 cup shredded coconut
1/8 tsp salt

**Filling:**
1-1/2 cups raw honey
1-1/2 cups coconut butter
1 cup coconut oil
5 cups frozen raspberries
6 Tbsp tapioca starch
1-1/2 tsp vanilla extract
1/4 tsp salt
Raspberries, fresh, for garnish
Thick coconut flakes, for garnish

1.  Place the jars of coconut oil, coconut butter, and raw honey in a pan with very hot water to let them soften.
2.  To prepare the crust, preheat your oven to 325°F. Strain dates and place in a food processor or high-powered blender with melted coconut oil. Blend for 30 seconds or so until a chunky paste forms. You may have to stop and scrape the sides if you are using a blender, and the oil will not completely mix with the dates, but the crust will still turn out fine.
3.  Combine coconut flour, shredded coconut, and salt in a bowl. Add date paste and mix thoroughly.
4.  Place mixture into the bottom of an 8" spring-form pan, pressing mixture down evenly. Use a small spatula to clean up the top edge around the sides of the pan, where the filling will meet the crust.
5.  Bake for 30-35 minutes, until the crust browns and hardens a little bit. The texture will still be soft until it finishes cooling. Set aside while you make the filling.
6.  To make the filling, combine the raw honey, coconut butter, coconut oil, and frozen raspberries in a saucepan on low heat. Stir until the raspberries are no longer frozen and the mixture is warm, about 5 minutes.
7.  Transfer to a blender and add the tapioca starch, vanilla extract, and salt. Blend on high for about a minute, until completely mixed. Pour carefully into the spring-form pan on top of the crust.
8.  Set in the refrigerator undisturbed for at least 12 hours to allow the cake to cool and harden. When it is solid, carefully remove the spring-form pan.
9.  Decorate the top of the cake with coconut flakes and fresh raspberries.

# Kelly Lamb
### HILLIARD, OH

Moving to a Paleo lifestyle has only affected me in positive ways!

I'm a reformed low-fat, high-carb, non-red-meat eater. I've had digestive issues since childhood. At age 19, I was diagnosed with recurring attacks of acute pancreatitis caused by unknown reasons, but doctors thought it had something to do with my diet of processed foods. I was inspired to learn to cook to manage the pancreatitis, but no amount of whole-grain, non-fat, all-natural, organic clean eating solved the problem. In 2011, after reading *The Paleo Solution*, I gave Paleo a try. I took baby steps to remove gluten-containing grains and legumes from my diet, and I now enjoy a life free of GERD, pancreatitis, and hypoglycemia.

Paleo has opened up a new world of foods to me, such as liver, sardines, fermented foods, and meats like bison and lamb. My previous diet of poultry, salad, and oatmeal rarely challenged me to get creative in the kitchen and left me weak in the gym. These days, I love being in the kitchen experimenting with foods that are new to my palate. I'm able to lift heavier weights and compete in endurance events without straying from Paleo.

I love Paleo so much that I was inspired to build my own Paleo recipe website (www.CookingKelly.com). I use produce found seasonally in my region and healthy meats that are raised humanely. I hope my recipes will inspire others to live a healthier life by cooking more meals at home.

# Baked Pork Ribs

Estimated Prep Time: 5 minutes
Estimated Cooking Time: 2 hours
Servings: 2 to 4

1 large slab of pork ribs (3-4 lbs)
1 Tbsp honey

**Rub ingredients:**
1 Tbsp smoked paprika
1 tsp salt (I use Himalayan Pink Salt)
1/4 heaping tsp unsweetened dark
  chocolate powder
1/4 tsp ground ancho chili pepper
1/4 heaping tsp ground cinnamon
1/8 tsp ground cardamom

1. Coat ribs in honey (no more than 1 Tbsp).
   Be sure to spread evenly. Sprinkle rub
   onto ribs and rub in.
2. Wrap ribs completely in foil so they
   steam while they bake.
3. Bake at 350°F for 2 hours or until easy to
   pull meat apart with a fork.

Before I was introduced to Paleo, my proteins consisted of chicken, eggs, and beans. Going Paleo has given me a chance to branch out into cooking other meats. I'm sort of a "clean slate!" I wanted to try making ribs that have a great flavor without needing to be covered in sugary sauces. **THESE RIBS GOT THE HUSBAND SEAL OF APPROVAL FOR A FOOTBALL SUNDAY—NO SUGARY SAUCE NEEDED!**

speaking to groups both large and small about the benefits of going Paleo, hosting Paleo cooking demos, writing for several online publications, and working on my own books. These are but a few components of the arsenal of Paleo tools I use on a daily basis to support my long-term goal: to change the way America eats by implementing the real Paleo diet.

I went Paleo in 2005. In 2004, I contracted a parasite during an Ironman race, which catapulted my lifelong battle with stomach issues to an all-new extreme. I sought medical advice and accepted my prescription for Flagyl right away, but continued to feel worse and worse. After six months, I was at my wit's end. I began to research online and, through trial and error, discovered I had developed a gluten intolerance. Despite six months spent visiting doctors and specialists (none of whom asked anything about my diet) and more than one trip to the ER, I was left to my own devices to solve my health problems.

I'd previously always eaten a "healthy" diet with lots of veggies, fruit, whole grains, legumes (lots of soy and peanuts when I was vegan for two years!), and organic dairy. I was a "fit" age-group athlete on the outside, but on the inside, my GI system seemed to be rapidly progressing from the mildly annoying stomachaches I'd had for years, to being doubled over in pain after every snack or meal!

I stumbled across *The Paleo Diet,* read it, and began following it right away. I felt better in three days. I wrote to Dr. Cordain to thank him for his work and tell him what a gift it had been to discover and share it with my clients. He wrote back, and the rest is history!

I've been on this track since 2005, and there's no reverting. Paleo living is the way to live!

I'm Nell Stephenson, the original "Paleoista" (www.Paleoista.com). I'm one of the collaborators of *The Paleo Diet Cookbook* with Dr. Loren Cordain and Lorrie Cordain, and the author of *Paleoista: Gain Energy, Get Lean and Feel Fabulous with the Diet You Were Born to Eat.*

"Paleoista" is a term I coined, trademarked, and used in the title of my first solo book, and it comes from a hybrid of two words: Paleo and fashionista. My goal is to demonstrate that true Paleo doesn't have to be all about being a caveman!

My work includes counseling clients online across the globe on their newly "Paleo-ized" diets,

# Paleoista's Wild Salmon, Eggs, Kale & Avocado

Estimated Prep Time: 5 minutes
Estimated Cooking Time: 10 minutes
Servings: 2

1 Tbsp coconut oil
6 oz wild king salmon, sashimi grade
2 large eggs from pastured hen
2 cups shredded organic kale
1/2 fresh lemon, juiced
1 small avocado, sliced

One of the easiest ways to approach "true" Paleo is to realize that **FOOD IS FOOD, ANY TIME OF DAY.** Toss the idea of making the "most important meal of the day"—breakfast—with grains and dairy and you're off to a good start. Here is one of my favorite breakfasts, featuring a lovely balance of wild protein and fresh, local veggies, complemented by the satiating addition of some natural fat. Sometimes simple really is best!

1. Heat coconut oil in a skillet over medium-high heat.
2. Sear salmon 1 minute on each side and remove from pan.
3. Crack eggs in the skillet and cook over easy.
4. Toss the kale with lemon juice and massage well with your hands.
5. Divide the kale in half and place on two plates.
6. Top with the salmon, egg, and avocado.

# Kelly Bejelly
PORTLAND, OR

I came to the Paleo diet because I needed to find a way to heal the damage being a nine-year vegetarian had done to my body. I was suffering from anxiety, panic attacks, and depression. I was also very overweight and pre-diabetic. I'm a huge proponent of natural medicine, and the thought of taking insulin every day, as well as the fear of going blind or losing one of my limbs, made me take the leap and try the diet.

It's amazing that by removing grains, legumes, and most sugars from my diet, I was able to find mental balance and lose 50 pounds. It's so true that food is medicine and that the body is an incredible organism that can heal when given the proper nourishment. I also attribute my quick pregnancy, despite my PCOS, to the diet.

My husband jumped on board when he started to see my health improvements, and for the first time in years he stopped battling constant heartburn and acid reflux. Like most men, he lost weight quickly and his physical endurance increased. As a result, he can mountain bike and ski longer.

We're raising our son on the diet, and he's a healthy, active toddler. A huge bonus to the diet is I don't have to deal with the "sugar" temper tantrums that some moms have to deal with, and he's a pretty mellow kid. Of course, he eats all of our bacon, but that's a price I'm happy to pay for the improvements in our overall health!

www.AGirlWorthSaving.net

# Paleo Cinnamon Square Crunch Cereal

Estimated Prep Time: 10 minutes
Estimated Cooking Time: 25 minutes
Servings: 8

1 cup coconut shreds
1/2 cup sunflower seeds
1/4 cup chia seeds
1 Tbsp cinnamon
1/4 tsp sea salt
1/4 cup maple syrup
1 egg

1. In a blender or food processor, add coconut shreds, sunflower seeds, chia seeds, cinnamon, and sea salt. Pulse until you have a flour.
2. Place flour in a small mixing bowl and add maple syrup and egg.
3. Blend well.
4. Scoop mixture onto a piece of parchment paper and cover with another piece of parchment paper.
5. Roll until you have a rectangle, roughly 8" x 10" and 1/4" thick.
6. Remove the top sheet and pre-cut the dough into 1/2" x 1/2" squares.
7. Place the parchment paper on a baking sheet and cook at 325°F for 20 to 25 minutes until dark brown.

# Keirsten Murphy
## PORTLAND, ME

Most recently, we've been learning how to forage and gather our own wild foods! To us, the "Paleo" lifestyle is about being in tune with where our food comes from, how it's grown or raised, the nutrition it provides us, and the manner in which it is harvested. We eat mostly organic, free-range chicken thighs, grass-fed beef, organ meats, pastured eggs, pastured butter, raw dairy, pastured pork, and a huge variety of organic, mostly locally grown vegetables. We collect our own spring water, as well as sap water for our own maple syrup.

My immediate family is my partner and me. We are both active, we love the outdoors, and we love to eat good food. I enjoy cooking, and, well, he doesn't exactly enjoy the cleanup part, but hey, that's the deal! We live in Portland, Maine, where fresh, local food is abundant, especially in the spring and summer when wild food is growing and farmers markets begin to pop up everywhere.

We also love entertaining friends and family. My nine-year-old nephew Connor and my two nieces, Audrey (five) and Quinn (two and a half), come over for dinner often, so I try to make new, tasty foods that they will like. They love my lettuce tacos! Audrey calls them "salad tacos with tomatoes." I love when kids are excited about healthy food!

Adopting more of a "Paleo-ish" diet was a starting point for my partner and me. We first cut out gluten, then other refined and overly processed grains, then refined sugars. From there, we found other resources to support our venture of living a life from more of an ancestral or evolutionary context.

We also eat wild rice, sweet potatoes, organic potatoes, buckwheat, and other gluten-free, non-GMO grains. I know most "Paleo-goers" probably shudder when I say that, but my philosophy regarding a Paleo-ish diet is more in line with Weston A. Price's philosophy: eating foods that proved to produce healthy offspring for generations and generations. "Paleo" was our starting point. From there, we developed our own template, using the framework set forth by Paleo leaders such as Mark Sisson and Loren Cordain. We are still learning about seasonal wild foods that are available to us and we continue to incorporate them into our everyday meals.

www.KeirstensKitchen.com

# Cookie Dough Balls

Estimated Prep Time: 15 minutes
Estimated Cooking Time: N/A
Servings: 10

5 fresh black figs, well ripened
2 Tbsp coconut oil
1/2 cup raw almond butter
1 cup chopped raw hazelnuts (use food processor)
1/2 cup dried, unsweetened coconut flakes
1/4 cup maple syrup
1/4 cup coconut flour
1/2 cup almond meal
1-1/2 Tbsp vanilla extract

**EVERY PALEO-GOER LOOKS FOR A QUICK, HEALTHY BUT RELATIVELY SWEET SNACK FROM TIME TO TIME,** and these are perfect! Make a small batch for you and your family to nibble on for dessert, or make a large batch and bring it to a barbeque. Raw ingredients, no dairy, and naturally sweet figs and maple syrup make these a go-to snack, especially for kids.
www.KeirstensKitchen.com

1. Melt coconut oil.
2. Mash figs and mix with oil.
3. Mix all remaining ingredients in with oil and figs. Mixture should form a cookie-dough texture. If too dry, add tablespoons of water, 1 Tbsp at a time, while mixing well.
4. Roll into small, bite-sized balls.
5. Can keep in refrigerator; balls will be more dough-like if brought to room temperature before eating.

# Kristen Mcdade

HOUSTON, TX

I'm 42 years old, newly married, and mother to a 16-year-old daughter, Josie. I'm a commercial real estate broker in one of the busiest markets in the country, so you could say I'm short on time! I've battled weight issue most of my life and have Hashimoto's thyroidism (for which I've taken Synthroid for years), along with arthritis and a history of migraines.

Shortly after my husband and I were married, I started to get very tired and my weight began to increase. I could tell that my thyroid was out of whack as I was feeling angry and anxious. My joints were hurting and making it too difficult to exercise. I was getting worse by the day and could not figure out what to do. I felt miserable, and at 41 years old could not imagine living my life like this. I made a call to the man I call "my witchdoctor" for an initial visit and some natural help, but he couldn't see me for six months. I took the appointment and a package came in the mail the next day. I didn't recall ordering the book in the box, *It Starts With Food*, but I liked the cover and sat down and read it. The whole thing, in one go. I started following the plan it outlined to a "t," and this evolved into my Paleo life.

After 30 days, I had huge energy, I felt clear-headed, my joints were feeling better, my skin was glowing, and I was losing weight! I decided I was going to keep going, and loved it. After four months I had lost about 25 pounds and decided it was time for some CrossFit. My joints are not quite ready for it, but I still eat the Paleo way and I'm slowly getting more active by the day. My daughter was so impressed by all my progress that she wrote a book about Paleo for her sophomore project, and got it published! She is my inspiration. She powers through water polo, and is smart as a whip, and I want to make her proud!

I do get off track from time to time—but I know the course to get back to good, natural, healthful eating of nature's real food.

# Fast Green Easy

Estimated Prep Time: 15 minutes
Estimated Cooking Time: 5 minutes
Servings: 2

1 large or 2 smaller broccoli heads,
  trimmed to florets
Several asparagus spears, cut to bite-size pieces
Handful grape tomatoes, halved
1/2 ripe avocado, diced
Salt and pepper to taste
Juice of 1 lemon
1 Tbsp your favorite homemade Paleo mayo

I go home every day for a fast lunch and to let out my sweet doggy. **ALWAYS LOOKING FOR OPTIONS AND BORED OF LUNCHTIME SALADS, ONE DAY I JUST THREW TOGETHER WHAT I HAD ON HAND.** This was a change from a bowl of guac, plus my doggy loves to snack on asparagus! It holds me over till dinnertime, and provides plenty of green veggies without the usual lettuce salad for lunch.

1. Steam or boil broccoli florets and asparagus pieces for 5 minutes.
2. While that's going, toss diced avocado and tomatoes in a bowl.
3. Drain asparagus and florets (cut a little smaller if you like), and add to avocado and tomatoes while a little warm.
4. Add mayo, salt, pepper, and lemon juice. Start tossing, lightly pressing your utensils as you go. The creaminess of the avocado mixes with the lemon juice and mayo and creates a lovely background for the salad.

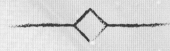

Note: You can add some grilled chicken for a protein, or any other veggies that suit you. Crumbled bacon is also tasty here!

Paleo is still a relatively new lifestyle for my family and me. When pregnant with my first child (who is now almost seven), I began to learn more about nutrition and how to feed her to give her the best foundation possible. Over the years, I added to my knowledge with individualized learning, formal training as a nutrition educator, and many, many hours in my in-laws' kitchen, where I learned to cook and enjoy Indian food. They have passed on to me some of their incredible wisdom about food, culture, and tradition, as well as a love and appreciation for great-tasting food.

They don't follow a Paleo lifestyle, but many of their cultural and culinary traditions align with those of the Paleo community. Many Indian foods can be made Paleo with a few simple substitutions, and the cuisine is rich in spices, fresh vegetables, and quality meats and seafood. My in-laws' wisdom, combined with my knowledge about nutrition, has transformed my kitchen and my family. My goal is to continue learning and applying new ideas, ingredients, and techniques to nourish my family while still honoring the culture and traditions of my own family and those of my Indian husband.

My family has benefitted from our transition to a Paleo lifestyle with improved nutrition, an increased awareness about how sleep and activity affect our health, and a focus on more-holistic means of treating illness. For me, that's the most important part of a Paleo lifestyle: awareness. What is in the food I am eating? Where did it come from? What is best to feed my family? What do I put on my body? What other factors influence my health? I agree with the underlying principles of the Paleo lifestyle, but I also believe in a sustainable balance between those principles and the culinary and eating traditions of my and my husband's ancestry.

More than anything, I love being part of a community that doesn't think it strange that I drink bone broth or that I render my own tallow. I also love the support and encouragement I get from other Paleo lifestylers who recognize our incredible individuality when it comes to nutrition and lifestyle choices. We are a community of many personalities, preferences, and biological constitutions, and my family is just one part of an amazing group of humans who are striving for the best that food and life have to offer.

www.HalfIndianCook.com

# Stovetop Tandoori Chicken

Estimated Prep Time: 30 minutes
Estimated Cooking Time: 30 minutes
Servings: 6 to 8

2-1/2 - 3 lbs. boneless, skinless free-range chicken thighs,
  cut into bite-size pieces
3-4 Tbsp tandoori masala (choose one that is free of sugar,
  artificial colors, and preservatives)
Coconut oil for cooking
1 tsp jeera mix (1 part whole fenugreek, 2 parts whole black
  mustard seeds, 8 parts whole cumin; mix well and store in an
  airtight container)
1 medium yellow onion, sliced
1 cinnamon stick
8-10 curry leaves
Thumb length of fresh ginger, peeled and minced
8-10 cloves garlic, minced
1/2-1 tsp haldi (turmeric)
Ground mircha (chili powder), to taste (we like it hot!)
Sea salt, to taste
1 small bunch cilantro, rinsed and chopped

1. Trim chicken thighs of large pieces of fat and/or bone
   and cut into bite-sized pieces.
2. Rinse well with cold water; drain and pat dry with paper towels.
3. Put chicken in a mixing bowl and sprinkle liberally with
   tandoori masala (3 to 4 Tbsp). Mix well so that the spices cover
   all of the chicken pieces.
4. Cover and either let it sit on the countertop for 20 to 30 minutes
   or refrigerate for up to 4 hours. The longer it marinates, the
   tastier it will be!
5. In a large skillet or pot over medium heat, melt enough coconut
   oil to cover the bottom completely, about 1/8 inch deep.
6. When oil is hot, add jeera mix; let seeds pop for a few seconds
   and then add sliced onions. Stir well.
7. Let onions cook until they begin to soften, stirring often so they
   don't brown too much or burn.
8. After a few minutes, add cinnamon stick and curry leaves.
9. When onions are almost done cooking, add in the ginger,
   garlic, ground mircha, and haldi. Stir well.
10. Add in chicken, stirring to coat it in the sauce. Add some salt to
    taste (just a little—you can add more later if needed).
11. Cover chicken and let it cook until done, about 30 minutes.
    Check every once in a while to stir it and make sure it isn't
    sticking to the bottom of the pan. You'll know it's done when the
    meat is soft and splits easily when pushed with a wooden spoon.
12. When meat is cooked completely, add the cilantro, stir well, and
    remove from heat.
13. Serve and enjoy!

**MY INDIAN HUSBAND AND I LOVE TANDOORI CHICKEN,** which, when done right, is one of the most delicious things on earth. In Indian restaurants, chicken is marinated in spices and (often) yogurt, then cooked in a tandoor (clay oven). The result is bright-red, smoky, juicy, spicy chicken.

My husband's auntie taught me how to make this stovetop version, which has become a favorite among our family and friends. My version is adapted to Paleo-friendly cooking ingredients, including coconut oil and spices that are free from sugar, artificial colors, and preservatives.

Note: If you want more sauce, keep it covered until it's done cooking. If you prefer it drier (which is how we like it), take the cover off about halfway through cooking.

## Sarah Fragoso
CHICO, CA

Living a Paleo lifestyle has changed so many aspects of our family's lives beyond simply what's for dinner. The Fragoso family views life in general differently than we used to. Five years ago, I couldn't have imagined that we would be where we are today. Never mind the fact that we've overcome illness and fatigue, and forget the part about losing fat and gaining muscle. Let's also look past the fact that we now have boundless energy to play together, laugh together, and love each other. All of these changes have been astounding and wonderful, but the preeminent difference in our lives as a result of living a Paleo lifestyle is our newfound awareness of the world around us.

Eating "clean" for our family has evolved into so much more! I'm now aware of and care deeply about where our food comes from. We try diligently to support our local organic farmers and grass-fed meat suppliers, and we take our children to farmers markets and to local farms where they are practicing sustainable agriculture. We have jumped in with both feet and are now proud owners of several chickens who provide us with our eggs; we are growing our own small garden; and my toaster has been replaced with a slow cooker filled with mineral-rich bone broth. Our children dig outside in the dirt with us, play in the sunshine, and spend less and less time with electronic gizmos and gadgets.

These are all steps we have taken to not only maintain our health but to support our environment and our local economy, and to show our children where real food comes from. Most importantly, we now understand that there is hard work and yet plenty of reward involved in trying to live the best life possible!

I am forever grateful for these opportunities and my eyes have truly been opened to so much more than the need to find the right "diet." My hope is that as we continue on our journey, our lives will influence others in a positive way and that more families will join us and reap benefits simply by starting where we did—by eating the foods our bodies were intended to eat, moving our bodies in the ways in which they were built to move, sleeping enough, playing a lot, and loving deeply. As always, enjoy!

www.EverydayPaleo.com

# Lamb Sliders with Ginger Cilantro Aioli and Sweet Potato "Buns"

Estimated Prep Time: 25 minutes
Estimated Cooking Time: 25 minutes
Servings: 12

**Sweet Potato Buns:**
3 medium-to-large white sweet
   potatoes, peeled and sliced
   1/4" thick (lengthwise)
1 Tbsp coconut oil
Sea salt, to taste
Granulated garlic, to taste
Black pepper, to taste
Oregano, dried, to taste
Italian seasoning

**Ginger Cilantro Aioli:**
2 Tbsp minced fresh cilantro
2-3 Tbsp fresh lime juice
1 cup homemade mayo
1 tsp minced fresh jalapeño,
   seeds removed
1 tsp grated fresh ginger

**Lamb Sliders:**
2 lb ground grass-fed lamb
1 tsp sea salt
1 tsp black pepper
2 garlic cloves, minced
1 Tbsp lard, butter, or ghee

**Optional garnishes for sliders:**
Romaine lettuce
Red onion
Tomatoes, sliced
Dill pickles

**Sweet Potato Buns:**
1. Preheat oven to 375°F.
2. Lightly season sweet potatoes with the sea salt,
   garlic powder, pepper, oregano, and Italian seasoning.
3. Place the sweet potatoes on a baking sheet lightly coated
   with coconut oil and bake at 375°F for approximately 10
   minutes, then flip them over and cook for another 10 to 15
   minutes or until done. Watch closely and once they are
   brown, remove them from the oven!
4. Let finished sweet potatoes rest for a few minutes, and
   in the meantime prepare the aioli and lamb sliders.

**Ginger Cilantro Aioli:**
1. Mix all of the above ingredients together in a bowl and
   place in the refrigerator while you prepare the sliders.

**Lamb Sliders:**
1. Season the ground lamb with the salt, pepper, and garlic;
   mix together and with your hands and form your sliders.
   The meat will make total of 12 sliders, about 1/2" thick and
   about 4" across. Create more of an oval shape to fit the
   sweet potato bun.
2. Heat the lard, butter, or ghee in a large skillet over medium-
   high heat and cook the sliders for about 3 to 5 minutes per side.
   Lamb cooks quickly, so watch closely and don't overcook!

To assemble the sliders, spread some of the aioli onto the sweet
potato bun, add a slider, and garnish as you like.

# Maureen Smithe

CHICAGO, IL

My husband Chris introduced our family to the Paleo lifestyle a couple years ago. As a captain in the Army, a rugby player, and a CrossFitter, he's always been very active and health-conscious. But several years ago he developed some minor health issues that were starting to interfere with his day-to-day life, and his doctors wanted him to rely on a lifelong supply of prescriptions to control the symptoms. In hindsight, it's shocking that Chris's doctors never once suggested a change in diet. Sure enough, he skipped the pills and opted for Paleo, and his health has been great ever since.

As the primary cook in our household, I was reluctant to make the switch to Paleo because I enjoy trying new recipes and techniques. But I agreed to give it a chance because I knew my husband's health literally depended on it. Much to my surprise, it really hasn't been too difficult. Many people think a Paleo diet is very restrictive, but I've found it to be quite the opposite. I'm always coming up with new recipes for vegetables, and we cut out a lot of foods that didn't make us feel very good anyway (like pasta and heavy bread dishes). Of course, we splurge every now and then (Chicago has some great pizza places we just can't resist, and I love baking), but Paleo has taught us about moderation and the importance of paying attention to our body's cues.

RUTHIE HAUGE PHOTOGRAPHY

# Fudgy Paleo Pops

Estimated Prep Time: 15 minutes
Estimated Cooking Time: 5 minutes
Servings: 10 to 12

3 cans full-fat coconut milk
3 Tbsp vanilla extract
1-1/4 cup pure maple syrup
3/4 cup cocoa powder

My husband started the Paleo diet after joining a CrossFit gym, and **HIS OUTLOOK ON FOOD AND LIFE IMPROVED DRASTICALLY**. I prepare most of the meals for our family, and the kids and I are now on a mostly Paleo diet due to his influence. It's been a lot of fun coming up with new ways to enjoy familiar foods. My husband loves this dessert, and so do the kids!
**www.HomeMadeMothering.com**

1. Whisk all ingredients in a medium sauce pan. Bring to a simmer over medium heat and whisk well.
2. Remove from heat and bring to room temperature. Cool in refrigerator for at least 2 hours.
3. Pour into popsicle molds and freeze.
4. Enjoy!

# EPILOGUE: The Paleo Lifestyle

"When we try to pick out anything by itself, we find it hitched to everything else in the universe."

—John Muir

This has been a story about the connections formed in and around eating. We have seen the ways that the sharing of food has shaped our evolution, and how eating together forges bonds that are powerful and healthful. We have taken a hard look at the industrial food system, from the middlemen to the factory farms, and how we can thwart it by eating real food. We have explored alternatives to shopping at supermarkets, discovering that we can still be hunter-gatherers of a sort, and maybe gardeners if that suits us better.

But food is not the only axis around which the world rotates. The Paleo lifestyle is about more than just the Paleo diet. Even with the most perfect diet in the world, you can still be unhappy.

If you peel back the layers, the reason we choose to eat well in the first place is because we truly desire to feel happy, satisfied, and well. By focusing our attention on happiness, we also support our health. Happiness has been scientifically proven to be boosted by a variety of behaviors, and many of them are lifestyle factors that are embraced by the Paleo lifestyle. The happiest people are typically generous, express gratitude, have an open mind, and are willing to try new things. We can also improve our overall satisfaction with life by having goals, getting a good night's sleep, and cultivating some sort of spirituality. Not surprisingly, spending less time stressed out behind the wheel of a car and more time in the company of close friends and loved ones are significant ways to boost our happiness levels.

In addition to supporting happiness, the Paleo lifestyle is also about taking time to relax and appreciate the small things, cultivating patience, and enjoying the way things unfold when we step away from artificial controls. Prehistoric humans didn't have television, the internet, or video games. Instead, they observed the plants, animals, and earth that surrounded them. It's easy to fall into the trap of trying to force things, to make things happen, and to try and bend the universe to our will. This is a futile struggle at best. Letting go of our need to know the outcome of every situation gives us the opportunity to be surprised, to be vulnerable, to be human.

Our ancestors were not lone hunters, and as a result, we developed as a social species. If we are to look to the lifestyles of ancient people as inspiration for our modern diet, we also have to recognize the importance of community and building close relationships with others. In the past, these relationships were born of necessity out of the shared goal to survive, but today we have to come together willingly. This is both a challenge and an opportunity to do something that has never been done before. In the midst of a modern world that has increasingly isolated us from one another, we can set aside the technology that has been inserted between our interactions and choose to live lives that are more authentic and fulfilling.

Movement, both playful and intentional, also defined our ancestral experience. Building shelters, tracking game, and defending against enemies would require extreme levels of exertion, but, as evidenced by modern hunter-gatherers, time was also given to dancing, games, and play. The concept of "working out" would be unbelievable to a Paleo human, since walking on a treadmill might trick your heart into beating faster but it does little to quicken your mind or stir your creativity. Playing sports with your friends, engaging in activities like hiking or mountain climbing, and doing cartwheels with your kids are all things that put us back in contact with the way we were designed to move, exercising our bodies, minds, and spirits without concern for the calories burned.

By creating a way of living and loving instead of just following a diet plan, you can build a foundation of health, happiness, and well-being that resists the manipulations of Big Food, protects against the diseases of the modern world, and becomes an inspiration for others. While this way of living might start with changes on your plate, look for ways to allow those changes to ripple outward, spreading the word of real, authentic living to your family, friends, community, and world. The problems we face as a society are many and varied, but the complex web of relationships that surround food offer us an opportunity to start solving them, one bite at a time.

CHAPTER 1 RESOURCES:

Gowdy, John. "Hunter-gatherers and the mythology of the market." Libcom.org. http://libcom.org.

Kaplan, Hillard and Michael Gurven. "The Natural History of Human Food Sharing and Cooperation: A Review and a New Multi-Individual Approach to the Negotiation of Norms."
http://www.anth.ucsb.edu/faculty/gurven/papers/kaplangurven.pdf

McMillan, Sherrie. "What Time is Dinner?" History Magazine.
http://www.history-magazine.com/dinner2.html

Klein, Maury. "The Technological Revolution." Foreign Policy Research Institute.
http://www.fpri.org/footnotes/1318.200807.klein.techrevolution.html

"TV dinner," Wikipedia. https://en.wikipedia.org/wiki/TV_dinner

"Microwave Ovens." IEEE Global History Network.
http://www.ieeeghn.org/wiki/index.php/Microwave_Ovens

"Nielsen Estimates 115.6 Million TV Homes In The U.S., Up 1.2%." Nielsen.
http://www.nielsen.com/us/en/newswire/2013/nielsen-estimates-115-6-million-tv-homes-in-the-u-s---up-1-2-.html

Grotticelli, Michael. "Living room TV is now the "second" screen,"
Broadcast Engineering Blog.
http://broadcastengineering.com/blog/living-room-tv-now-second-screen

Stiglitz, Joseph. "The Book of Jobs." Vanity Fair.
http://www.vanityfair.com/politics/2012/01/stiglitz-depression-201201

Hagenbaugh, Barbara. "U.S. manufacturing jobs fading away fast." USA Today.
http://usatoday30.usatoday.com/money/economy/2002-12-12-manufacture_x.htm

"Data tables for the overview of May 2012 occupational employment and wages." U.S. Bureau of Labor Statistics.
http://bls.gov/oes/2012/may/featured_data.htm#largest


CHAPTER 2 RESOURCES:

Hyman, Mark. "How Eating at Home Can Save Your Life." Huffington Post.
http://www.huffingtonpost.com/dr-mark-hyman/family-dinner-how_b_806114.html

The National Center on Addiction and Substance Abuse at Colombia University. "The Importance of Family Dinners VI." September 2010.
http://www.casacolumbia.org/upload/2010/20100922familydinners6.pdf

Hammons, Amber J and Barbara H Fiese. "Is Frequency of Shared Family Meals Related to the Nutritional Health of Children and Adolescents?" Pediatrics. 127.6 (2011): e1565-1574. http://pediatrics.aappublications.org/content/127/6/e1565.full

Eisenberg, Marla E, Rachel E Olson, Dianne Neumark-Sztainer, Mary Story, and Linda H Bearinger. "Correlations Between Family Meals And Psychosocial Well-being Among Adolescents." Archives of Pediatrics and Adolescent Medicine 158.8 (2004): 792-796.
http://archpedi.jamanetwork.com/article.aspx?articleid=485781

"American Time Use Survey." U.S. Bureau of Labor Statistics.
http://www.bls.gov/tus/charts/leisure.htm

Sapolsky, Robert M. Why zebras don't get ulcers : a guide to stress, stress related diseases, and coping. New York: Holt, 2013.

Newman, Leigh. "Life Changes: How to Create New Habits." Huffington Post.
http://www.huffingtonpost.com/2012/11/26/life-changes-how-to-createhabits_n_1970105.html

Oliver G, J Wardle, and EL Gibson. "Stress and food choice: a laboratory study." Psychosom Med. 62.6 (2000): 853-65.
http://www.ncbi.nlm.nih.gov/pubmed/11139006

"Study: Family dinnertime feeds the company's bottom line." BYU News.
http://news.byu.edu/archive08-Jun-dinner.aspx

Jerath, R, J Edry, V Barnes, and V Jerath. "Physiology Of Long Pranayamic Breathing: Neural Respiratory Elements May Provide A Mechanism That Explains How Slow Deep Breathing Shifts The Autonomic Nervous System." Medical Hypotheses 67.3 (2006): 566-571.
http://www.ncbi.nlm.nih.gov/pubmed/16624497

"Majority of Americans not Meeting Recommendations for Fruit and Vegetable Consumption." Centers for Disease Control and Prevention.
http://www.cdc.gov/media/pressrel/2009/r090929.htm

Liddell, Henry G, and Robert Scott. A Greek-English Lexicon, revised and augmented throughout by Sir Henry Stuart Jones with the assistance of. Roderick McKenzie. Oxford: Clarendon Press. 1940. Perseus Digital Library.
http://www.perseus.tufts.edu/hopper/text?doc=Perseus:text:1999.01.0126

Meiselman, Herbert L. and MacFie H.J.H. Food choice, acceptance, and consumption. London: Springer. 1996.

Wardle J, M-L Herrera, L Cooke, and EL Gibson. "Modifying children's food preferences: the effects of exposure and reward on acceptance of an unfamiliar vegetable." European

Journal of Clinical Nutrition. 57.2 (2003): 341-348.
http://www.nature.com/ejcn/journal/v57/n2/abs/1601541a.html

"CE Expenditure Tables." Bureau of Labor Statistics.
http://www.bls.gov/cex/csxstnd.htm

CHAPTER 3 RESOURCES:

"Supermarket Facts Industry Overview 2011 – 2012." Food Marketing Institute.
http://www.fmi.org/research-resources/supermarket-facts

Greenberg, Melanie A. "Ten Ways Your Local Grocery Store Hijacks Your Brain."
Psychology Today.
http://www.psychologytoday.com/blog/the-mindful-self-express/201203/
ten-ways-your-local-grocery-store-hijacks-your-brain

Chicago Historical Society. "Grocery Stores and Supermarkets." The Electronic
Encyclopedia of Chicago.
http://www.encyclopedia.chicagohistory.org/pages/554.html

Nestle, Marion. Food Politics: How the Food Industry Influences Nutrition and
Health. Berkeley: University of California Press, 2002.

"Richard Nixon: Address to the Nation Announcing Price Control Measures."
The American Presidency Project. http://www.presidency.ucsb.edu/ws/?pid=3868

Wyant, Sara. "Memories of Agriculture Secretary Earl Butz." Agri-Pulse.
http://www.agri-pulse.com/uploaded/021008.pdf

Pollan, Michael. "What's Eating America." Smithsonian Magazine.
http://www.smithsonianmag.com/people-places/presence-jul06.html

University of North Carolina at Chapel Hill. Oral History Interview with Lauch
Faircloth. Interview I-0070. Southern Oral History Program Collection (#4007)
in the Southern Oral History Program Collection, Southern Historical Collection,
Wilson Library. July 16, 1999.
http://docsouth.unc.edu/sohp/I-0070/excerpts/excerpt_1029.html

"The United States Summary Information." Environmental Working Group Farm
Subsidy Database. http://farm.ewg.org/region.php

Moisse, Katie. "Baby Boomers Living Longer, Not Healthier." ABC News.
http://abcnews.go.com/blogs/health/2013/02/05/
baby-boomers-living-longer-not-healthier/

Battistoni, Alyssa. "America Spends Less on Food Than Any Other Country."
Mother Jones.
http://www.motherjones.com/blue-marble/2012/01/america-food-spending-less

"Agriculture Fact Sheet." Agriculture Council of America.
http://www.agday.org/media/factsheet.php

CHAPTER 4 RESOURCES:

Bledsoe, Brandon. "The Significance of the Bear Ritual Among the Sami and Other Northern Cultures." The University of Texas at Austin. http://www.utexas.edu/courses/sami/diehtu/siida/religion/bear.htm

Raff McCaulou, Lily. "Why hunting your own dinner is an ethical way to eat." Eatocracy. http://eatocracy.cnn.com/2012/07/02/55-why-hunting-your-own-dinner-is-an-ethical-way-to-eat/

Hynek, Jenni. "Cost Analysis: Hunted Venison Vs Store Bought Beef," The Midwest Texan. http://themidwesttexan.blogspot.com/2010/08/cost-analysis-hunted-venison-vs-store.html

Sisson, Mark. "On the Problems of Cultivated Fruit." Mark's Daily Apple. http://www.marksdailyapple.com/on-the-problems-of-cultivated-fruit/

Carlsen, Monica H, David R Jacobs, Laura Sampson, Steinar Dragland, Siv K Bøhn, Kari Holte, Bente L Halvorsen, Rune Blomhoff, Katherine M Phillips, Walter C Willett, Nega Berhe, Ingrid Barikmo, Chiho Sanada, Yuko Umezono, Haruki Senoo, and Carol Willey. "The Total Antioxidant Content Of More Than 3100 Foods, Beverages, Spices, Herbs And Supplements Used Worldwide." Nutrition Journal 9.1 (2010): 3. http://www.nutritionj.com/content/9/1/3

"Organic Tomatoes Contain Higher Levels of Antioxidants Than Conventional Tomatoes, Study Suggests." ScienceDaily.com. http://www.sciencedaily.com/releases/2012/07/120703120630.htm

Irving, Miles. "Foraging is more than just a middle-class leisure pursuit." The Guardian. http://www.guardian.co.uk/commentisfree/2006/sep/12/comment.ruralaffairs

Von Baeyer, Edwinna. "The Development and History of Horticulture." Encyclopedia of Life Support Systems. http://www.eolss.net/Sample-Chapters/C09/E6-156-07-00.pdf

Isabella, Jude. "The Edible Seascape." Archaeology, Volume 64.5 (2011). http://archive.archaeology.org/1109/features/coast_salish_clam_gardens_salmon.html

Roach, John. "Was Papua New Guinea an Early Agriculture Pioneer?" National Geographic News. http://news.nationalgeographic.com/news/2003/06/0623_030623_kukagriculture_2.html

"Victory Gardens History." Victory Gardens 2008+. http://www.sfvictorygardens.org/history.html

Siegelbaum, Portia. "Cuba's Urban Agrarians Flourish." CBS. http://www.cbsnews.com/2100-202_162-4154650.html

## PALEO RADIO

MAGAZINE

modern day primal living

← HOSTED BY: TONY FEDERICO

PALEO MAGAZINE RADIO BRINGS YOU PALEO
NUTRITION, EXERCISE, AND LIFESTYLE PERSPECTIVES
FROM BOTH THE EXPERTS AND THE EVERYDAY.

**paleomagonline.com/radio**

ALSO
ON: